# Table of C

# CliffsNotes™
# Creating a
# Budget
## by Ro Sila

## IN THIS BOOK

- Evaluate your spending habits
- Create a budget that puts you on track to a secure financial future
- Revise and update your goals as your circumstances change
- Reinforce what you learn with CliffsNotes Review
- Find more budgeting information in CliffsNotes Resource Center and online at www.cliffsnotes.com

IDG Books Worldwide, Inc.
An International Data Group Company
Foster City, CA • Chicago, IL • Indianapolis, IN • New York, NY

IDG
BOOKS
WORLDWIDE

## About the Author

Ro Sila has been an independent writer and editor since 1974, specializing in business and self-improvement issues. She has won writing awards and has been published in anthologies, newspapers, and magazines.

## Publisher's Acknowledgments

### Editorial

Senior Project Editor: Pamela Mourouzis
Senior Acquisitions Editor: Mark Butler
Associate Acquisitions Editor: Karen Hansen
Copy Editor: Patricia Yuu Pan
Technical Editors: John Eisenbarth, J. Patrick Gorman

### Production

Proofreader: York Production Services
Indexer: York Production Services
IDG Books Indianapolis Production Department

**CliffsNotes Creating a Budget**
Published by
IDG Books Worldwide, Inc.
An International Data Group Company
919 E. Hillsdale Blvd.
Suite 400
Foster City, CA 94404
www.idgbooks.com (IDG Books Worldwide Web site)
www.cliffsnotes.com (CliffsNotes Web site)

Library of Congress Catalog Card No.: 99-64201
ISBN: 0-7645-8512-6
Printed in the United States of America
10 9 8 7 6 5 4 3 2 1
1O/QZ/QY/ZZ/IN
Distributed in the United States by IDG Books Worldwide, Inc.
Distributed by CDG Books Canada Inc. for Canada; by Transworld Publishers Limited in the United Kingdom; by IDG Norge Books for Norway; by IDG Sweden Books for Sweden; by IDG Books Australia Publishing Corporation Pty. Ltd. for Australia and New Zealand; by TransQuest Publishers Pte Ltd. for Singapore, Malaysia, Thailand, Indonesia, and Hong Kong; by Gotop Information Inc. for Taiwan; by ICG Muse, Inc. for Japan; by Norma Comunicaciones S.A. for Colombia; by Intersoft for South Africa; by Eyrolles for France; by International Thomson Publishing for Germany, Austria and Switzerland; by Distribuidora Cuspide for Argentina; by LR International for Brazil; by Ediciones ZETA S.C.R. Ltda. for Peru; by WS Computer Publishing Corporation, Inc., for the Philippines; by Contemporanea de Ediciones for Venezuela; by Express Computer Distributors for the Caribbean and West Indies; by Micronesia Media Distributor, Inc. for Micronesia; by Grupo Editorial Norma S.A. for Guatemala; by Chips Computadoras S.A. de C.V. for Mexico; by Editorial Norma de Panama S.A. for Panama; by American Bookshops for Finland. Authorized Sales Agent: Anthony Rudkin Associates for the Middle East and North Africa.
For general information on IDG Books Worldwide's books in the U.S., please call our Consumer Customer Service department at **800-762-2974**. For reseller information, including discounts and premium sales, please call our Reseller Customer Service department at **800-434-3422**.
For information on where to purchase IDG Books Worldwide's books outside the U.S., please contact our International Sales department at 317-596-5530 or fax **317-596-5692**.
For consumer information on foreign language translations, please contact our Customer Service department at **800-434-3422**, fax **317-596-5692**, or e-mail rights@idgbooks.com.
For information on licensing foreign or domestic rights, please phone **650-655-3109**.
For sales inquiries and special prices for bulk quantities, please contact our Sales department at 650-655-3200 or write to the address above.
For information on using IDG Books Worldwide's books in the classroom or for ordering examination copies, please contact our Educational Sales department at **800-434-2086** or fax **317-596-5499**.
For press review copies, author interviews, or other publicity information, please contact our Public Relations department at **650-655-3000** or fax **650-655-3299**.
For authorization to photocopy items for corporate, personal, or educational use, please contact Copyright Clearance Center, 222 Rosewood Drive, Danvers, MA 01923, or fax **978-750-4470**.

**Note:** This book is intended to offer general information on personal finance. The author and publisher are not engaged in rendering legal, tax, accounting, investment, real estate, or similar professional services. Although legal, tax, accounting, investment, real estate, and similar issues addressed by this book have been checked with sources believed to be reliable, some material may be affected by changes in the laws and/or interpretation of laws since the manuscript in this book was completed. Therefore, the accuracy and completeness of the information provided herein and the opinions stated herein are not guaranteed or warranted to produce particular results, and the strategies outlined in this book may not be suitable for every individual. If legal, accounting, tax, investment, real estate, or other expert advice is needed or appropriate, the reader is strongly encouraged to obtain the services of a professional expert.

# INTRODUCTION

Like it or not, you deal with money every day. Some people deal with it better than others do. The difference is in their money-management skills. You're not born with these skills; you learn them. And improvement comes with practice.

Because you picked up this book, I know that you're at least somewhat motivated to start living on a budget so that you can take control of your spending and start saving. You've come to the right place! CliffsNotes *Creating a Budget* takes a practical look at the many phases of creating a budget. You'll find information that you can use to pursue better management of your money so that it can go further and lead to investments that provide greater financial security.

## Why Do You Need This Book?

Can you answer yes to any of these questions?

- Do you need to learn about creating a budget fast?
- Don't have time to read 500 pages on budgeting?
- Do you find that you don't know where your money goes?
- Do you want to be able to meet your financial goals and have a secure financial future?

Then CliffsNotes *Creating a Budget* is for you!

## How to Use This Book

How to use this book is really up to you — you need to find the approach that works best for your own situation. The important thing is to get started. Unless you *do something* to take control of your money, nothing will happen.

Here are some ways that I recommend you search for the information you need:

- Use the index at the back of the book.

- Flip through the book and look for your topic in the running heads across the tops of the pages.

- Check the table of contents at the front of the book.

- Look through the "In This Chapter" list at the beginning of each chapter.

- Flip through the book until you find what you need — the book is organized in a logical, task-oriented way.

For additional sources of information about budgeting, check the CliffsNotes Resource Center at the back of the book.

To alert you to especially important information in the book, the following icons appear in the margins next to certain paragraphs. Here's what the icons mean:

This icon highlights words of wisdom and suggestions that can save you time and energy and perhaps spare you a headache or two.

This icon gives you a heads-up on potentially dangerous situations. Skipping this information could be hazardous to your financial health.

This icon points out information that's too important to forget.

# Don't Miss Our Web Site

Keep up with the exciting world of personal finance by visiting the CliffsNotes Web site at www.cliffsnotes.com. Here's what you find:

- Interactive tools that are fun and informative

- Links to interesting Web sites

- Additional resources to help you continue your learning

At www.cliffsnotes.com, you can even register for a new feature called CliffsNotes Daily, which offers you newsletters on a variety of topics, delivered right to your e-mail inbox each business day.

If you haven't yet discovered the Internet and are wondering how to get online, pick up *Getting On the Internet*, new from CliffsNotes. You'll learn just what you need to make your online connection quickly and easily. See you at www.cliffsnotes.com!

# CHAPTER 1
# "YOU ARE HERE" IN YOUR FINANCIAL LIFE

## IN THIS CHAPTER

- Figuring out what you're worth
- Looking at your goals
- Setting your time line for reaching those goals

Whether you're in Manhattan, Montana, or Mozambique, every map you come across will have a "You Are Here" arrow. Why? Because you can't get to where you want to be if you don't know where you are.

Your budget is a financial map to help you reach your financial goals, and it's useless unless you know where you are now and where you want to go. Determine your current financial situation by taking a thorough survey of your current financial status. This chapter shows you how.

Committing time to build your financial plan may be your most important investment in your future.

## Figuring Out What You're Worth

When budgeting, people usually think of "worth" as cash in the form of salary, savings, checking accounts, and so on. But you can make a number of decisions about anything you have that has value, and each of those decisions affects your financial worth.

## Income

How much money do you take home after federal taxes, state taxes, local taxes, and social security deductions? (Most people budget on a monthly basis, but if you get paid weekly or semimonthly, you may want your budget to reflect that income pattern.)

You may want to include temporary, part-time, or seasonal income in your budget. On the other hand, you might choose to treat that extra income like "found money" and put it directly into your savings or investment plan. With the benefits of compound interest, such mini-investments may have a significant impact on your future. I discuss *compounding* (interest that is paid on interest already earned) later in the book so that you truly understand the benefits of forgoing small pleasures now for giant rewards later.

## Savings

How much money do you have in a bank, savings and loan, or credit union savings account(s)? Do you have a money market account? Certificates of deposit? A Christmas Club account? For the purposes of figuring your financial worth, your savings list includes all *liquid assets,* or assets that you can readily turn into cash. (If you find that you have too many accounts in too many places, try consolidating them into fewer accounts. By consolidating, you can save fees, make tracking your assets easier, and make more money with accounts that pay higher interest.)

## Other assets

The "other assets" category itemizes your less-liquid holdings. Some of these assets may not figure into your monthly budget, but you need to be aware of them. By evaluating these assets carefully, you may find that you can make them serve your purposes better by *liquidating* them (converting them into cash) and applying their value in another category.

Other assets include stocks, bonds, mutual funds, retirement funds, life insurance, real estate, and other investments, such as vehicles (land, water, *or* air!), jewelry, and collectibles (like stamps or antiques).

Calculate your financial worth in the following worksheet.

**My Net Worth as of** _____

**Cash**

Checking account(s)                    _____

Savings account(s)                     _____

Money market account(s)                _____

Certificate(s) of deposit              _____

Other                                  _____

**Stocks, Bonds, and Mutual Funds**

Stocks                                 _____

Bonds                                  _____

Mutual funds                           _____

Commodities                            _____

Securities                             _____

Options                                _____

Other                                  _____

**Retirement Funds**

IRA(s) or Keogh       _____

401(k)       _____

Company pension plan       _____

Company savings plan       _____

Profit-sharing plan       _____

ESOP       _____

Other       _____

**Real Estate**

Equity in main residence       _____

Equity in vacation home(s)       _____

Equity in co-owned property       _____

Equity in rental property       _____

Other       _____

**Insurance**

Annuities, surrender value of       _____

Life insurance, cash value of       _____

**Personal Property**

Automobile(s)       _____

Boat(s)       _____

Recreational vehicle(s)       _____

Furniture, appliances, etc.       _____

Antique(s)       _____

Art: Painting(s), sculpture(s), etc.    _____

Collectibles: Stamps, coins, etc.    _____

Gold and/or silver    _____

Jewelry    _____

Other _____    _____

**Other**

_____    _____

_____    _____

_____    _____

As you remember other assets, return to this worksheet and enter their values, adding more lines as necessary.

## Setting Your Goals

One reason some individuals and families find it hard to set goals is that Americans generally are not good at looking at money in terms of long time lines. When you buy something that you don't really need because it costs "only" $30 a month, you're ignoring the total cost, which includes interest.

When you think about savings, you may see saving $30 a month as an awfully slow way to accumulate assets because you ignore interest compounding (discussed in Chapter 9). But saving is like the woman who, at age 47, hesitated to start medical school because she would be 51 by the time she got her degree. She finally decided to pursue her dream when her counselor pointed out that she would be 51 in four years, whether or not she went to medical school.

Setting goals is more than just writing down a dollar amount. It's a way to ensure that you will not only enjoy your dreams but also enjoy the pursuit itself and the forward steps you take along the way.

Goals are usually divided into short-term, mid-term, and long-term goals. These terms mean different things to each budget planner, depending on where you are on your life's path.

As the 21st century approaches, the average life expectancy in the United States is about 80 years, up almost 68 percent since the turn of the last century. During your lifetime, what you *want* — and what you *need* — are different at each stage of your life. Meeting goals in the short term not only reinforces that you can meet your longer-term goals but also (happily) reinforces your determination to do so.

**Remember**

Budgeting is not denying yourself pleasures and happiness. Rather, it is creating a financial plan that ensures that you'll have a joyful life at every age. Consider, for example, the current trend toward designer coffee. If you pay $3.75 to $5.50 every workday for 48 weeks a year, that little pleasure will cost you $900 to $1,320 a year! Add an expensive gourmet roll to that, and the amount can double. Five minutes after drinking either the latte or the company mud-brew, can you really recall what either tasted like? Get something memorable for your money!

### Short-term goals

You can set short-term goals for as soon as next week or as far away as next year. These goals may include paying for a vacation, buying a new stereo, or being able to attend your brother's wedding on the other side of the country. Or they may be stepping stones on the way to longer-term goals, such as accumulating a down payment for a home or car or starting a child's college fund.

The good news is that the dollar amount you need to have to meet these goals will not grow appreciably due to inflation. The bad news is that the "free" money you'll add to your fund from interest payments will be less than for longer-term goals.

Fill in your own short-term goals in Table 1-1. (The first three items are examples to help get you started.)

### Table 1-1:    My Short-Term Goals

| Goal | Goal Date |
|------|-----------|
| Save for car down payment | _____ |
| Start house fund | _____ |
| Save share of parents' anniversary party | _____ |
| _____ | _____ |
| _____ | _____ |
| _____ | _____ |
| _____ | _____ |
| _____ | _____ |

## Mid-term goals

Mid-term goals are usually defined as one- to five-year goals. These goals might include saving up a down payment on a vacation home or boat, going back to school, and meeting interim goals on your way to meeting your long-term retirement goals.

Both the negative effects of inflation and the positive effects of compounding interest are greater for these goals than for your short-term goals.

Fill in your own mid-term goals in Table 1-2.

**Table 1-2: My Mid-Term Goals**

| Goal | Goal Date |
|------|-----------|
|      |           |
|      |           |
|      |           |
|      |           |
|      |           |

## Long-term goals

Your long-term goals are five-year or longer plans. These goals are for long-term plans such as retirement. Your retirement savings plan might include intermediate goals for 5, 10, 15, 20, and so on years.

As you meet each goal on your way to your long-term goals, your resolve to meet the next goals will be more firm. But your goals may need to be updated. Changes in the goals of individual family members may necessitate revising the family's goals. Career changes, health problems, and responsibility for extended family members are other reasons your long-term goals may need revising. Winning the lottery might change your time line on some goals, too!

Remember

All news that impacts your financial picture — good and not-so-good — requires you to go back to your financial road map to see whether you're still heading toward your goals.

In Table 1-3, write your own long-term goals and the dates by which you hope to achieve them.

**Table 1-3:    My Long-Term Goals**

| Goal | Goal Date |
|---|---|
| | |
| | |
| | |
| | |
| | |

# Determining How Much Your Goals Will Cost

The following questions can help you decide how much you need to save to meet each goal according to its particular time frame:

- How much would this goal cost if you bought/paid for it today?

- Using an appropriate rate of inflation, how much will the goal cost on its due date?

   Using historical rates of inflation, you can apply that average rate over the term of the goal to determine what the cost will be on the goal's due date.

   If your goal has its own inflation rate — for example, the cost of education is rising at a faster rate than overall inflation — use that rate instead of the standard rate of inflation.

   Base your calculations on the highest estimated costs. That way, you won't be caught short. You can always transfer the "extra" to your retirement plan.

- What average after-tax rate of interest do you expect to earn on your savings for this goal?

■ How much will compounding your earned interest add to your savings for this goal?

Table 1-4 shows you how a relatively small investment of $50 per month can grow into a major asset with the help of compounding interest.

**Table 1-4: The Impact of Compounding Interest**

| Year | At 0% Interest | At 12% Interest | At 13% Interest |
|------|---------------|-----------------|-----------------|
| 5 | $3,000 | $4,083 | $4,194 |
| 10 | $6,000 | $11,502 | $12,201 |
| 15 | $9,000 | $24,979 | $27,485 |
| 20 | $12,000 | $49,462 | $56,662 |
| 25 | $15,000 | $93,942 | $112,354 |
| 30 | $18,000 | $174,748 | $218,663 |
| 35 | $21,000 | $321,547 | $421,592 |
| 40 | $24,000 | $588,238 | $808,953 |
| 45 | $27,000 | $1,072,734 | $1,548,371 |
| 50 | $30,000 | $1,952,916 | $2,959,812 |

Notice the difference that even 1 percent interest makes in the accumulation of dollars. So start your savings plan immediately and reach your goals even faster!

# CHAPTER 2
# LOOKING AT WHERE YOUR MONEY GOES

## IN THIS CHAPTER

- Evaluating your spending habits
- Putting your spending into categories
- Learning about the tools for tracking your spending
- Identifying how you think about money and spending

In your financial life, you may be spending (or paying bills) until you have no more money. Then you wait for your paycheck and start the process all over again. That approach may have worked (although not all that well) back in the days when you were collecting an allowance from Mom and Dad. It may have worked even in college when your dorm fees included food — at least you wouldn't freeze or starve to death. As time goes on, though, this "system" becomes less and less sound.

This chapter helps you figure out where you're currently spending your money so that you can lay the groundwork to set up your budget. A budget enables you to make wiser, more informed decisions about your spending.

A budget doesn't cause stress; the *lack* of a budget causes stress!

## Keeping a Spending Diary

Keeping a spending diary helps you determine how you're currently spending your money on a day-to-day basis. For your diary, use a small notebook that fits in your pocket or purse. Carry it everywhere. Attach a pen or pencil so you have no excuse for not writing down every purchase you make. Every day. Every cent. Keep your spending diary for at least a month.

On each new page, write the day and date. Record your purchases whether you spent cash, used a credit card, or added to a tab. At the end of each day, total your expenses. To make this exercise even more useful, you can divide your weekly after-tax income by 7, write that amount on each day's page, and at the end of the day figure out whether you spent more than you made that day.

There are three ways to keep your diary:

- Use two columns: one for the amount and one for a description.

- Decide how many categories you want, and then draw and label your columns (you'll probably use two facing pages). Categories might include groceries, restaurant meals, snacks, transportation, clothing, and telephone calls.

- Draw fewer columns for wider categories, such as food, transportation, and miscellaneous. Write a key in the front or back of your notebook so that you can keep track of the items within each category. For example, under food you can use G for groceries, R for restaurant meals, and S for snacks.

    Table 2-1 shows an example of this type of spending diary. The codes for Transportation are P for parking and G for gasoline; the miscellaneous codes are C for clothing and T for telephone calls.

**Table 2-1:    My Spending Diary for (Today's Date)**

| Food | Transportation | Miscellaneous |
|------|----------------|---------------|
| R $10.50 | B $5.25 | C $39.00 |
| S $2.50 | G $39.48 | T $2.75 |
| G $33.88 | | |

If your miscellaneous column adds up too fast, you probably need more categories. And if you find that you're altering your spending habits as you keep your diary, don't write your totals until the end of the month so that your diary reflects your true spending habits, not the habits you *think* you should have.

# Using Other Tools to Track Your Spending

Did you realize that your bank and credit card statements can help you create a budget? Rather than just checking to make sure that the amounts are correct, you can use these records to see how much money you spend in each category. Use the same key that you used for your spending diary.

Using the information that you gather, you can create a budgeting worksheet. Pencil and paper are fine, but if you have a home computer, financial software has become so inexpensive and so easy to use that you may choose to keep track of your spending habits that way.

The time you invest now to gather information and set up your budget pays off in easier tracking and decision-making later. You've already made the decisions about your money; you just have to apply them.

## Bank records

Every month, your bank, credit union, or other financial institution sends you a list of how much you put into your account and how much you spent out of it. Bank records are a good place to use different-colored highlighters to put your expenditures in categories: To start, try green for savings and red for impulse purchases.

If you have a computer and a modem, you can use online banking. Many banks have set up systems where you can see current and even past records by using the Internet. You can find out whether a specific check has cleared. You can check your current balance. You can check your records when it's convenient for you rather than waiting for the postal service to deliver your statement.

The easier you make it to keep track of your finances, the more likely you are to do it.

To make your life easier, consider using your computer to set up automatic payments for such expenses as

■ Mortgage

■ Utilities

■ Telephone

■ Credit cards

■ Savings

Your bank doesn't have to offer online banking for you to be able to pay your bills online. It's not even necessary that those companies you want to pay be able to accept online payments; if they can't receive electronic payments, checks will be mailed to them. You sign up with an online service, pay a monthly fee (which may or may not be worth the convenience), and then provide information about your checking account and the bills you want paid. The service either electronically transfers money from your account to each creditor or removes the money from your account and mails a check to the creditor.

## Credit card statements

Those handy reports that you get every month recording your credit card activity also help you draw your financial map. Signing on the dotted line to make a purchase is so easy that many people do so much more often than they should. Again, using highlighters, mark each purchase to be tallied in a specific category.

## Budgeting software

Computers can do many things for you. Luckily, keeping track of your money is one of them! Programs like Quicken, Budget, and Microsoft Money are inexpensive yet flexible. These programs do the basics, like keeping track of your check record and balancing your checkbook. But that's just the beginning.

Like the paper worksheet in Table 2-2, later in this chapter, budgeting software creates a budget for you according to your specifications. Even better than automatically calculating totals as you enter amounts, the software enables you to move items from category to category. (For example, you may want to move restaurant meals from the Food category to the Personal category.) You can also create what Quicken calls *supergroups*. For example, you can put housing, transportation, and food under a supergroup called "basic."

Why are supergroups important? Because you don't have to add up the same group totals repeatedly. On the other hand, you still have the total for smaller groups without having to separate and add them up one by one.

Flexibility allows you to reorganize your budget so that it gives you the information you want. Once you've set up a budget, you aren't stuck with it. And as your situation changes, you can customize your budget to reflect your new reality.

Depending on the software package you buy, you can compare your forecasted spending with actual spending in any category, know when expenses are due with the use of a financial calendar, monitor your loan payments, manage your investments, and create reports and graphs to show how you're progressing toward your goals.

Don't put off budgeting because you don't have a computer. Software is nice, but not necessary.

If you have a friend or family member who is an expert in one software package, buy it! You'll have your own software coach.

## Evaluating Where Your Money Goes

With your spending diary in hand, you have the information you need to set up your budget. Knowing where your money goes can help you keep it from going!

Table 2-1 is a budgeting worksheet that shows you what your spending history looks like. Using the past six months of bank and credit card records, figure your expenses in each category. For items that fluctuate, such as food, add up your six-month total (SMT). Then double that amount to get your yearly cost. Divide your SMT by 6 for your monthly cost for that item. Divide your SMT by 26 to calculate your weekly cost. Prepare to be shocked at how much you're spending in some categories!

## Table 2-1:    My Budget Worksheet

| Expense | Weekly | Monthly | Yearly |
|---|---|---|---|
| **Housing** | | | |
| Rent or mortgage | | | |
| Condo association dues | | | |
| Maintenance | | | |
| Property taxes | | | |
| Insurance | | | |
| Furniture and appliances | | | |
| **Utilities** | | | |
| Gas | | | |
| Electricity | | | |
| Water | | | |
| Garbage | | | |
| Sewer | | | |
| Telephone | | | |
| **Food** | | | |
| Groceries | | | |
| Eating out | | | |
| **Transportation** | | | |
| Automobile lease/ payment 1 | | | |
| Automobile lease/ payment 2 | | | |
| Licensing | | | |
| Insurance | | | |
| Maintenance | | | |
| Gasoline | | | |

*Continued*

**Table 2-1: My Budget Worksheet** *(continued)*

| Expense | Weekly | Monthly | Yearly |
|---|---|---|---|
| **Transportation** | | | |
| Public transportation | | | |
| Parking/Tolls | | | |
| **Health** | | | |
| Doctor(s) | | | |
| Dentist(s) | | | |
| Medications | | | |
| Insurance | | | |
| **Education** | | | |
| Tuition/School fees | | | |
| Books and supplies | | | |
| School activities | | | |
| **Personal** | | | |
| Clothing | | | |
| Haircuts | | | |
| Cosmetics | | | |
| Pets | | | |
| Childcare | | | |
| Child support | | | |
| Allowances | | | |
| Gifts | | | |
| Donations | | | |
| Membership dues | | | |
| Magazine and newspaper subscriptions | | | |
| Laundry/Dry cleaning | | | |
| Other _____ | | | |

| Expense | Weekly | Monthly | Yearly |
|---|---|---|---|
| **Savings and Investment Contributions** | | | |
| Savings accounts | | | |
| 401(k) | | | |
| IRA(s) | | | |
| Stocks | | | |
| Mutual funds | | | |
| Bonds | | | |
| Other _____ | | | |
| **Credit and Loan Payments** | | | |
| Credit card 1 | | | |
| Credit card 2 | | | |
| Credit card 3 | | | |
| Department store card | | | |
| Gasoline card | | | |
| Student loan | | | |
| Other _____ | | | |
| **TOTAL EXPENSES** | | | |
| **Income** | | | |
| Wages, total | | | |
| Gratuities | | | |
| Dividends and interest | | | |
| Social security | | | |
| Pension | | | |
| Trust fund | | | |
| Royalties | | | |
| Child support paid to you | | | |
| Gifts | | | |
| **TOTAL INCOME** | | | |

Tip

You can add, subtract, or rearrange items to create a worksheet that fits your particular situation.

Now you know how much you're spending in each category. After you create a budget based on what you *want* to spend in each category and adjust your spending habits accordingly, you'll be able to tell when you overspend or underspend in a category. Neither situation is cause for despair or jubilation as long as your long-term expenditures stay within your personal range. If you consistently overspend, you may need to cut costs, or you may have underestimated your costs initially. On the other hand, if you consistently underspend your allowance in any category, you may be able to lower that budget item and reallocate the difference.

## Identifying Your Money Personality

The best-laid plans are worthless if you can't follow them. To find the best plans for *you* and help yourself stick to your budget, you need to understand how you feel about money and how you react to money matters. Figure out which of the following money personality types most accurately describes you:

- **Saver:** You have trouble spending money even when doing so is in your best interests.

- **Spender:** Your immediate reaction to available cash (or even available credit) is to figure out what you can buy with it. Sometimes you spend because you can't resist salespeople. You use credit if you don't have cash, with no concern for the long-term consequences of that debt.

- **Impulse buyer:** When you see something you like, you buy it without evaluating the purchase in terms of your long-range goals. Impulse buyers react to one or two types of items (whereas spenders buy everything!).

- **Cautious buyer:** You are a serious comparison shopper who may waste more time making a decision than the item is worth.

You need to understand not only your own money personality, but that of your spouse or partner as well. (As you teach your children about budgeting and saving, identify their money personalities, too.) Once you recognize your personality type, you can identify which habits you need to keep or change to reach your financial goals:

**Tip**

- You might think that a saver wouldn't have any changes to make. But you can actually save to the point of hurting yourself.

  For example, when Mrs. Brown moved in with her daughter, seven people from her workplace volunteered to help her move. Her new home was a three-hour round-trip drive from her old home. The truck rental contract called for a forfeit of the $45 deposit if the truck wasn't returned by 2 p.m., but included no added hourly rental charge as long as the truck was returned by 5 p.m.

  So with seven no-cost workers, Mrs. Brown hurriedly loaded the truck, left everything in the unattached garage at her daughter's home, and rushed back before the 2 p.m. deadline. In saving $45 (assuming that unskilled movers would make about $6 per hour), she "spent" about $126 (7 people x 3 hours = 21 hours x $6 per hour = $126) and had many expensive things stored in a garage without climate control. The two women — one 82 and the other 56 — had to move heavy furniture upstairs to get it into the house. Did Mrs. Brown "save"?

- A spender has more problems to overcome than the obvious. The attitude that any money available is available only to spend, rather than to put in savings, is its own problem. But it's not unbeatable. If you learn to stop, evaluate, consider alternatives, and make a decision instead of reacting to the desire to spend (or giving in to a sales pitch), you'll have a more secure financial future.

- An impulse buyer is similar to a spender. But an impulse buyer doesn't even have to "find" money available for spending. Just seeing something to buy is enough to bring out the wallet or credit card. The desirable habit to cultivate is the same as that for a spender. If you figure how many hours of after-tax income would be needed to buy an item, you can stop much of your impulse buying in its tracks. If you have a working stereo system, for example, is it really worth hundreds of work hours to replace it?

- Cautious buyers may waste both time and money. And time *is* money. A cautious buyer may spend too much time gathering information about various features and comparing prices and also incur the cost of phone calls and driving around. Even worse, a cautious buyer may not enjoy a purchase after making it if he or she sees the item on sale later. If you're a cautious buyer, use those good comparison-buying skills, but learn when enough information is enough to make a decision, and ignore any information that you gather after the purchase.

If you have a lot of trouble making a buying decision, you may not need to buy that item at all.

**CHAPTER 3**

# CREATING A BUDGET

## IN THIS CHAPTER

- Learning techniques to recognize *all* your expenses

- Categorizing your spending into essentials and nonessentials

- Recognizing that you have money available to start saving

In Chapters 1 and 2, you gathered and organized information so that you can create a realistic and workable budget. In this chapter, you'll use the information that you collected, making changes and fine-tuning so that your tools will work for you.

## Determining Your Essential Expenses: What You Need

*Essential expenses* are those obligations that you must pay regularly — usually monthly. *Fixed* essential expenses are the same month after month. They include the following:

- Rent or mortgage payment

- Insurance that you pay quarterly, semiannually, or annually

- Automobile payment

- Student loan payment

Although charitable contributions generally are not considered essential expenses, you can put those items in the essential category if you want to pay them regularly.

*Variable* essential expenses are due every month, but the amounts vary from month to month. In this category, you *prorate* (average) regular expenses to a monthly cost. Do so by figuring your yearly cost and dividing by 12 (if you're using a monthly budget) or 52 (if you're using a weekly budget).

Variable essential expenses include

■ Groceries

■ Utilities (gas, electricity, water, and so on)

■ Long-distance telephone expenses

■ Gasoline

■ Auto repairs and maintenance

■ Healthcare

■ Education costs

■ Haircuts, toiletries, and other personal care items

■ Savings for retirement

■ Savings for large expenses, such as furniture, appliances, and replacement automobiles

Remember

As you update your budget, you'll remove items such as student loans as you pay them off.

## Determining Your Nonessential Expenses: What You Want

After you pay your essential expenses, what you have left is your *discretionary income.* From that, you pay your nonessential expenses (and put the rest in savings and investments).

Nonessential expenses include the following:

- Books, magazines, and newspaper subscriptions
- Restaurant meals
- Movies and concerts
- Gifts
- Vacations
- Hobbies

Chapter 2 lists various money personalities. Your money personality identifies how you feel about money and spending. Recognizing your money personality — and the personalities of family members — helps you make better decisions about the spending that you've identified as discretionary.

In Table 2-1 back in Chapter 2, you discovered where your money went in the past. In creating your budget, you're looking toward the future. You want to determine which expenses that you listed as fixed really should be considered nonessential. You may be shocked at the total of these items, but don't be discouraged. You'll learn how to reduce your expenses in Chapter 5.

The whole point of a budget is to have a plan for your money *before* you spend it. Without a budget, you can leave the house with $200 in cash, come back five hours later, and be able to account for only half that amount. With a budget, you'll never do that again. More important, you'll be able to make firm spending decisions based on criteria that you have already set for yourself.

# Recognizing and Avoiding Hidden Expenses

Hidden expenses are those sneaky money-eaters that lurk everywhere. Knowing what and where they hide and how much they cost helps you cut them by avoiding the items to which they are attached.

This section identifies these hidden costs. Chapter 5 shows you how to cut them.

## Bank, ATM, and credit card fees

Hidden costs at banks, at ATMs, and on credit cards can quickly transfer your money from your pocket to an institution's profit statement. Be careful of the following:

- Annual fees
- Below-minimum-use and below-minimum-balance fees
- High interest rates
- Late-payment penalties
- Per-use fees

**Warning**

Read all change-of-terms inserts that you receive from banks, credit unions, credit card companies, and the like. The information that they contain may be a call to change how and where you do business.

Not knowing what fees you're liable for with your money-handling institutions is the same as using a credit card without knowing what rate of interest you're paying. If you don't carry a balance on your credit card, the interest rate is irrelevant. If you don't incur fees from your bank and so on, you don't care what that fee is, either. But you need to know what and how much they are so that you know what to do to avoid them.

## Gratuities and delivery charges

The more convenience services you use, the more you'll pay in gratuities and delivery charges. Having meals or groceries delivered is convenient and may save you time, but in addition to paying for what you eat, you pay for delivery costs and a tip for the delivery person — neither of which you can have for dessert.

Catalog shopping can save a lot of time, too, along with parking and car-use costs. An add-on cost, however, may be shipping charges (often unrecoverable if you return the item). You may need to pay insurance costs as well to protect against the item getting lost or damaged in transit. Plus, when you buy something in a store, you can inspect it before you take it home. And you can watch for sales.

This doesn't mean that you should always shop in stores; it just means that you need to know and compare the costs of various ways of taking care of your needs. If you use the time you save to earn more income, for example, the convenience may be worth the cost.

## Sales, luxury, and utility taxes

Not all items are taxed at the same rate. Grocery food, for example, is not taxed in some states and is taxed at a lower rate than other items in other states.

Legislatures have designated some items as luxury items. Liquor is a common example. In most places, the tax on soda is much lower than the tax on beer — even though you drink either one. The choices you make in what may seem to be the same category can lower these hidden costs. Read your receipts carefully. Some modern cash registers put added taxes next to the item purchased so that you can readily see how much you're paying for items for which substitutes may be available.

Choosing one item over another may not save you a ton of money, but making decisions about saving over and over can help put you on the path to financial security.

Utilities often have their own taxes and tax rates. Cutting a utility bill that is taxed higher than, for example, food results in double savings — on the item and on its tax cost. In Chapter 5, when you look for ways to lower expenses, you may find even lower-cost substitutes for some of these items.

## Factoring in Emergency Expenses

You don't want to panic every time the refrigerator breaks down or the dog eats spoiled food and has to go to the vet. Whether or not such items appeared in your assessment of your spending in Chapter 2 (refer to Table 2-1), emergencies will happen. The worksheet in Chapter 2 reflects what you spent in the past. The budget you'll create later in this chapter reflects that emergencies do happen, so you'll have savings put aside to pay for such contingencies.

You can move some items from the emergency category to a "savings for replacement" category by keeping track of those budget items. For example, one of the biggest money-eaters in the emergency category can be your automobile, especially if it isn't maintained properly and regularly.

Table 3-1 can help you keep track of your car's care and feeding. List all repairs, regular service (whether done at a service station or by you), and tire purchases. Review your car's service manual to be certain that you're following the manufacturer's recommendations.

## Table 3-1: Auto Maintenance: Major Repairs

| Date | Odometer Reading | Repair Description | Repair Warranty | Cost | Last Done |
|------|------------------|--------------------|-----------------|------|-----------|
|  |  |  |  |  |  |
|  |  |  |  |  |  |
|  |  |  |  |  |  |
|  |  |  |  |  |  |
|  |  |  |  |  |  |

When deciding which parts to buy, the existence of a warranty and its terms can be deciding factors. Keeping track of the life of the warranty helps you get your dollars' worth. If a shop wants to add chargeable parts or labor to those covered by the warranty, ask to see what needs to be replaced and why. And if the needed repairs are costly, you may want to get a second opinion from another mechanic.

Some warranties are prorated (the cost of wear and tear is deducted), and others offer replacements (you get a new tire or other part). Knowing what you're buying makes comparisons easier.

Keep similar records on major appliances and furniture. Table 3-2 shows you what information you need to plan replacement purchases.

**Table 3-2: Major Purchases/Replacement Needs**

| Item | Date Purchased | Warranty Length | Expected Life | Purchase Price | Replacement Cost | Expected Replacement Date |
|---|---|---|---|---|---|---|
| Answering machine | | | | | | |
| Central air conditioner | | | | | | |
| Clothes dryer | | | | | | |
| Clothes washer | | | | | | |
| Computer | | | | | | |
| Dishwasher | | | | | | |
| Furnace | | | | | | |
| Garage door opener | | | | | | |
| Lawn mower | | | | | | |
| Microwave | | | | | | |
| Printer | | | | | | |
| Refrigerator | | | | | | |
| Roof | | | | | | |
| Sofa | | | | | | |
| Stereo | | | | | | |

| Item | Date Purchased | Warranty Length | Expected Life | Purchase Price | Replacement Cost | Expected Replacement Date |
|------|----------------|-----------------|---------------|----------------|------------------|---------------------------|
| Stove | | | | | | |
| Sump pump | | | | | | |
| Television | | | | | | |
| Vacuum cleaner | | | | | | |
| Water heater | | | | | | |
| | | | | | | |
| | | | | | | |
| | | | | | | |

Now that you have an idea of how much money you need to keep in an account to be able to pay cash for these items as you need them, you can put these amounts in your budget. You may choose to save up the money for these items in your emergency fund, but I suggest that you set up a separate household expenses fund to cover them.

## Taking Taxes into Account

You may have noticed that Table 2-1 does not deal with income taxes. Most people have their taxes deducted from their paychecks and don't need to deal with them separately until they file their tax returns.

As your investment plans bring in more dividends and income, or you take on another job that doesn't deduct taxes, be sure to review your tax withholdings and adjust them as needed. Doing so prevents a big tax bill at the end of the year; you also avoid penalties.

If, however, you're getting refunds — especially large refunds (you get to define *large* for yourself) — you need to make adjustments so that the taxes you pay throughout the year better reflect your liability. A refund is *not* "found money"; it is money that you lent to the government without earning interest on it. You wouldn't put your money in a 0-percent-interest savings account, so don't loan the government money at no interest.

Reasons that you may be getting a refund include the following:

■ You haven't claimed the number of deductions to which you're entitled. Be sure to adjust your deductions as your family situation changes.

- You deliberately took fewer deductions because you expected to earn outside income from which deductions would not be taken; then you didn't earn that income.

- Your employer is deducting too much according to the number of dependents you're claiming, or you haven't updated your deductions as your circumstances have changed.

- You worked overtime. The tax table assumes that you were making that income every week, resulting in too much tax being withheld.

- You're itemizing deductions and have deductions such as healthcare costs and property tax deductions that aren't reflected in your withholding.

## Paying Yourself First

Paying yourself first is one of the best money-management decisions you can make. Simply put, paying yourself first means that you put money into a savings program to meet your short-term, mid-term, and long-term goals *before* you pay anything else — including your rent or mortgage! If you're living from paycheck to paycheck, you may think that you can't do this. But determining where you spend your money shows you how you can pay yourself first and gain many benefits.

One thing you discovered when you tracked how you spent your money in the past is that emergencies — real or imagined — always get paid somehow. If an insurance payment came due, for example, you scrimped on restaurant meals or entertainment so that you had enough money to pay that important bill *before* your insurance was canceled.

If you can "find" the money when you absolutely *must* have it, then you can live on less than you've been spending. The obvious conclusion is that you can put money aside for savings if you respect yourself enough to pay yourself first.

Chapter 5 goes into detail about lowering your expenses. For now, it's enough to identify the money that you didn't need to spend. Put that money in the savings category of your budget. When the insurance payment came due, for example, you told yourself that you didn't have money to spend on restaurant meals or movies. Isn't your future at least as important as paying for your insurance?

You'll find that when you have savings (and you *will*), the lowered stress, greater stability, feeling of financial security, and general well-being you enjoy are worth much more than the time and effort you invest in creating and maintaining your budget.

## Setting Up a Basic Budget

Back in Table 2-1 in Chapter 2, you figured out where your money has been going. Discovering and dealing with your spending personality type give you hints on how to change your habits to create a realistic budget and keep it up-to-date. This section shows you how to set up a budget that reflects the reality of your current financial life.

Remember that budgeting software, discussed in Chapter 2, can help you create and maintain your budget.

Table 3-3 is a sample budget to show you what your budget might look like. Using the information from your spending diary, insert the values for what you paid in each category last month in the Last Month Actual column. After you determine what you should be spending in each category, put those amounts in the This Month Budget column. At the end of another month, put the amount that you actually spent in each category in the This Month Actual column.

This budget leaves you space in the Over/Under column to compare each item's real value to its real cost. When you compile your budget, you want to be able to compare real versus projected values.

Note that these categories are not the same as those in Table 2-1. You'll determine which categories you need to include, so I want to show you how budget worksheets can vary. Choose categories that reflect *your* situation.

**Table 3-3:   My Monthly Budget**

| Expense | Last Month Actual | This Month Budget | This Month Actual | Over/ Under |
|---|---|---|---|---|
| **Housing and Utilities** | | | | |
| Mortgage or rent | $_____ | _____ | _____ | _____ |
| Homeowners' or condo assn. fees | $_____ | _____ | _____ | _____ |
| Home maintenance | $_____ | _____ | | |
| Electricity | $_____ | _____ | _____ | _____ |
| Gas | $_____ | _____ | _____ | _____ |
| Water | $_____ | _____ | _____ | _____ |
| Garbage removal | $_____ | _____ | | |
| Sewer fees | $_____ | _____ | _____ | _____ |
| Telephone | $_____ | _____ | _____ | _____ |
| *Subtotal, Housing and Utilities* | $_____ | _____ | _____ | _____ |

Often, your mortgage, property taxes, waste removal fees, and insurance are lumped together in one payment. Don't "charge" yourself twice if you pay these expenses as part of your mortgage payments.

| Expense | Last Month Actual | This Month Budget | This Month Actual | Over/ Under |
|---|---|---|---|---|
| **Food** | | | | |
| Groceries | $_____ | _____ | _____ | _____ |
| Restaurant meals | $_____ | _____ | _____ | _____ |
| *Subtotal, Food* | *$_____* | _____ | _____ | _____ |
| **Clothing and Shoes** | | | | |
| Adult 1 | $_____ | _____ | _____ | _____ |
| Adult 2 | $_____ | _____ | _____ | _____ |
| Child 1 | $_____ | _____ | _____ | _____ |
| Child 2 | $_____ | _____ | _____ | _____ |
| *Subtotal, Clothing and Shoes* | *$_____* | _____ | _____ | _____ |
| **Child Care** | **$_____** | _____ | _____ | _____ |
| **Insurance** | | | | |
| Auto | $_____ | _____ | _____ | _____ |
| Health | $_____ | _____ | _____ | _____ |
| Homeowner's/ Renter's | $_____ | _____ | _____ | _____ |
| Life | $_____ | _____ | _____ | _____ |
| Other | $_____ | _____ | _____ | _____ |
| *Subtotal, Insurance* | *$_____* | _____ | _____ | _____ |

*Continued*

| Expense | Last Month Actual | This Month Budget | This Month Actual | Over/ Under |
|---|---|---|---|---|
| **Healthcare** | | | | |
| Dentist | $_____ | _____ | _____ | _____ |
| Doctor | $_____ | _____ | _____ | _____ |
| Optometrist | $_____ | _____ | _____ | _____ |
| Other practitioner | $_____ | _____ | _____ | _____ |
| Eyeglasses, contacts | $_____ | _____ | _____ | _____ |
| Prescriptions | $_____ | _____ | _____ | _____ |
| Other | $_____ | _____ | _____ | _____ |
| *Subtotal, Healthcare* | $_____ | _____ | _____ | _____ |
| **Auto** | | | | |
| Payment 1 | $_____ | | | |
| Payment 2 | $_____ | _____ | _____ | _____ |
| Gasoline 1 | $_____ | _____ | _____ | _____ |
| Gasoline 2 | $_____ | _____ | _____ | _____ |
| Maintenance 1 | $_____ | _____ | _____ | _____ |
| Maintenance 2 | $_____ | _____ | _____ | _____ |
| Tolls | $_____ | _____ | _____ | _____ |
| Taxis and other public transportation | $_____ | _____ | _____ | _____ |
| *Subtotal, Auto* | $_____ | _____ | _____ | _____ |
| **Personal** | | | | |
| Charitable contributions | $_____ | _____ | _____ | _____ |
| Cosmetics | $_____ | _____ | _____ | _____ |
| Entertainment | $_____ | _____ | _____ | _____ |

*Continued*

**Table 3-3:   My Monthly Budget** *(continued)*

| Expense | Last Month Actual | This Month Budget | This Month Actual | Over/ Under |
|---|---|---|---|---|
| **Personal, continued** | | | | |
| Haircuts | $_____ | _____ | _____ | _____ |
| Magazines, newspapers | $_____ | _____ | _____ | _____ |
| Organization dues | $_____ | _____ | _____ | _____ |
| Vacations | $_____ | _____ | _____ | _____ |
| Other | $_____ | _____ | _____ | _____ |
| *Subtotal, Personal* | $_____ | _____ | _____ | _____ |
| **Savings and Investments** | | | | |
| Savings/Money market account | $_____ | _____ | _____ | _____ |
| Education fund | $_____ | _____ | _____ | _____ |
| Mutual fund | $_____ | _____ | _____ | _____ |
| New car fund | $_____ | _____ | _____ | _____ |
| New home fund | $_____ | _____ | _____ | _____ |
| Retirement fund | $_____ | _____ | _____ | _____ |
| Emergency savings account | $_____ | _____ | _____ | _____ |
| Other | $_____ | _____ | _____ | _____ |
| *Subtotal, Savings and Investments* | $_____ | _____ | _____ | _____ |

| Expense | Last Month Actual | This Month Budget | This Month Actual | Over/ Under |
|---|---|---|---|---|
| **Taxes** | | | | |
| Federal income tax | $_____ | _____ | _____ | _____ |
| State income tax | $_____ | _____ | _____ | _____ |
| Local income tax | $_____ | _____ | _____ | _____ |
| Social security tax | $_____ | _____ | _____ | _____ |
| Self-employment tax | $_____ | _____ | _____ | _____ |
| Property tax | $_____ | | | _____ |
| *Subtotal, Taxes* | *$_____* | _____ | _____ | _____ |
| **TOTAL EXPENSES** | **$_____** | _____ | _____ | _____ |
| **Income** | | | | |
| Gross wages 1 | $_____ | _____ | _____ | _____ |
| Gross wages 2 | $_____ | _____ | _____ | _____ |
| Interest income | $_____ | _____ | _____ | _____ |
| Alimony/Child support paid to you | $_____ | _____ | _____ | _____ |
| Other | $_____ | _____ | _____ | _____ |
| **TOTAL INCOME** | **$_____** | _____ | _____ | _____ |

**Difference between income and expenses (put shortages in parentheses)**

$_____    _____    _____    _____

Make sure to account for all your expenses, but put them in any category that makes your budget work for you. For example, you may want to put your homeowner's or renter's insurance under Housing and Utilities rather than under Insurance. Moving items to other categories will reflect how you spend your money; your budget will reflect how you want to allocate your resources. Also, as you recognize new items, add them to your budget.

Remember that budgeting software can automatically prepare reports for you. Putting some of this information in graph form may make it easier for you to make comparisons and see changes.

## Being Realistic

Remember that *a budget is just a piece of paper.* After spending this much time hearing about the benefits of creating and following a budget, you may find that statement shocking. But if your budget doesn't reflect reality and you can't live within the boundaries you set, it's useless.

How does a budget become and remain realistic? When the figures you enter in your budget reflect reality and not wishful thinking, when you're willing to spend time to update your budget regularly, and when you recognize that changes need to be made and make them.

Not being realistic has more consequences than a failed budget. Failure begets failure. If you allow yourself to stop planning realistically for your future, you'll be stressed and you'll waste time making decisions over and over because you don't have answers already in place.

## CHAPTER 4
# STICKING TO YOUR BUDGET

### IN THIS CHAPTER

- Understanding the role of self-discipline in financial planning
- Controlling your impulse spending
- Recognizing the people who can help you stay on course
- Dealing with emergency expenses
- Learning how to make using a budget a habit

Realizing that you need a budget, gathering your information, and putting that information into a usable form are giant strides toward securing your financial future. This chapter shows you how to build on the foundation that you established by creating a budget.

## Good Discipline Equals Good Budgeting

You have many good habits that took time to cultivate. Sometimes it's hard to remember them, because once you *have* a good habit, you don't really think about it until you start to lose it. Give yourself credit for developing habits such as these:

- I brush my teeth every day.
- I change the oil in my car regularly.
- I send birthday cards to my friends and family.
- I get to work on time.

In the interest of appreciating that you can learn budgeting habits, too, check off in the following list those good habits that you've already picked up:

❑ I pay my bills on time.

❑ I balance my checkbook.

❑ I compare prices when I shop.

❑ I verify the charges on my credit card statement.

None of these habits by themselves will make your life either wonderful or awful. But adding good habits on top of good habits improves your life immensely.

You can't just fling your old bad habits out the window. To learn to be an effective budgeter, you must coax yourself into developing good habits. Check off the following activities that you can accomplish:

❑ Recognize how budgeting benefits me

❑ Notice changes in my spending habits and decide whether the changes are good or bad

❑ Revise my budget when my circumstances change

❑ Seek help when I need more information

❑ Set aside time each week to review my budget

❑ Write down changes that I want to make instead of keeping them in my head

Failing to use and revise your budget has many drawbacks:

■ You waste the time that you already spent collecting data.

■ You miss out on the many benefits that budgeting brings to your financial life, such as the ability to use decisions you've made rather than react to situations.

- Your stress level rises.

- You don't feel good about yourself.

# Reining In Your Impulse Spending

If, every time you return from the store, you find that you have more items than you intended to purchase, you're not entirely at fault. Store managers have studied consumers for years. Stores purposely develop floor plans that tempt you to buy things you didn't know you wanted and expose you to as many buying opportunities as possible. For example, why is milk, probably the most purchased item in any grocery store, at the back of the store? Those wily store managers know that if you have to look at long aisles of tempting items going to and from picking up milk, your shopping cart will very likely have more than milk in it.

**Remember**

Don't confuse good buys with impulse purchases. If you find a closeout on something your family uses and you can use it all before it spoils, that's a good buying decision, unless it means that you can't pay another bill and will have to pay a penalty fee on that bill.

## Recognizing your triggers

Previously, you may not have thought of your purchases as being "triggered." But if the milk scenario seems familiar to you, then you have your own triggers. Common triggers are

- **Fatigue:** You've worked hard, so you feel that you deserve a treat.

- **Money in your pocket:** You have the cash to pay for it, so why not have a treat?

- **Depression:** You try to make yourself feel better by buying yourself a treat.

- **Elation:** You think that nothing can go wrong when you feel so good, so you have a treat.

- **Celebration:** You or your friend/sibling/cousin/college roommate *deserves* a nice present to celebrate a birthday/anniversary/new job.

- **Competition:** You have to give the nicest gift, or at least one that's as nice as so-and-so's.

- **The desire to impress someone:** You think, "Wait until so-and-so sees this!"

Ensuring your long-term financial health is the best "treat" you can give yourself!

You probably know the kinds of things you're most likely to purchase on a whim. Go to that area of your house and *write down* those things that you've purchased impulsively so that you can see how much money you've wasted by not making thoughtful decisions.

For example, are tools your weakness? Do you find it impossible to pass by a hardware store? Then take your survey in your workshop, garage, or toolshed. Or do you buy yourself clothes? Then go to your closet. See the jacket that you bought because the color is beautiful? Of course, you have nothing that goes with it. How many items did you buy on sale but don't really work well with the rest of your wardrobe?

Write down every item that falls into the impulse-spending category. You don't need to go through every door or find every impulse purchase, but do write down all the impulse buys that you find in plain sight.

You'll use the list that you make in the next section. If you're part of a couple or you're doing this exercise with your children, reassure everyone before you start this exercise that its only purpose is to gather information.

If you use your survey to find fault with your or others' purchases, you'll defeat the purpose and discourage helpful suggestions.

After you've compiled your list of impulse purchases, follow these steps:

**1.** Write an estimated cost next to each item.

**2.** Put a plus sign (+) next to anything you think you have used as much as you should have for the price. For example, you may have used your snow blower every time it snowed, but that may mean that each five-minute snow-removal job has cost you $87 — no + there. And don't forget the cost to insure that expensive piece of equipment.

**3.** Put an asterisk (*) next to each item for which you could have purchased a reasonable substitute at a lower cost. I'm not talking about something that arbitrarily went on sale, but something for which a small investment of time would have resulted in paying a much lower price.

**4.** Next to the asterisk, write the price you think that you could have paid for a reasonable substitute. (Don't put garage-sale or second-hand-sale prices here — you have no guarantee that you would have found a comparable substitute.)

Don't ignore small impulse purchases. Although you may not have included those items in this list, you purchase them more often, so they add up quickly.

### Focusing on your goals

In Chapter 1, you made a list of your short-term, mid-term, and long-term goals. Retrieve that list now. You've gathered other information since then, so you'll probably want to revise the list before you work on eliminating impulse spending.

Now look at your revised goals list. Starting at the top of your list, apply the "overspent" amount from your impulse-buying list to paying for your goals, whether your goals are to pay off your debts, save more, start investing, or purchase something that you really need or want. You may need to take more than one overspent amount to make up one goal amount. Don't bother to prioritize your goals here; you just want to know how many goals you could have checked off your list if you hadn't made impulse purchases. For example, not buying that snow blower might have paid for two car payments.

## Stopping yourself from making a purchase

Now that you recognize what makes you indulge in impulse spending and what the payoff can be when you make informed purchases based on your financial goals, you can control your triggers. Do so by making conscious decisions *before* the temptation to buy reaches out to grab you.

Setting your "stop" triggers doesn't mean that you never get to treat yourself. If the supermarket is your downfall, for example, give yourself a set amount to spend any way you like. After a few trips to the store during which you can't decide which one treat you want, you'll find that you don't want any of them all that much!

If, like me, your impulse triggers go off in a type of store that sells big-ticket items, again give yourself a "treat budget." If you don't have enough money to buy what you want today, you can save up your treat allowance until you have enough money in that "account." But you don't get to buy now and pay with your future allowance!

# Rounding Up Your Support Team

All kinds of people and organizations are available to help you meet your goals. In the case of people, you need to know *why* they want to help you, how much time and energy they can offer, and what their individual money personalities are. You may want to review the section on identifying money personalities at the end of Chapter 2 before you assign helping roles to your support team.

## Spouse/Significant other

The best way to work as a team with your spouse or significant other is to agree on your goals and the prioritization of those goals. You may have to compromise on individual goals in order to reach your goals as a couple or family.

Often, one partner is a better money manager than the other. That partner may be better at resisting temptation, computing amounts, dividing long-term goals into mid-term and short-term goals, setting priorities, budget balancing, and so on. Or one partner may be better at some activities, while the other handles the remaining tasks.

The secret to a good partnership is agreeing to goals and how you're going to reach those goals. Then each partner does the best job possible for his or her responsibilities. In spite of the word *partner,* you may decide to give one person more authority than the other — as long as you both agree on who should have more authority when it comes to financial matters, and you remember that financial security, not being in charge, is your goal.

As time goes on and changes need to be made, use the same negotiating and compromise that brought you as far as you are to help you set up a new system.

## Children

If you have children, you certainly want to help them learn how to handle money. Keeping children involved in the budgeting process helps them learn the financial lessons that they need to know at each stage in their lives.

For example, when Charles's children started getting allowances, he deducted 10 percent from each child's allowance. Needless to say, the first few deductions caused much upset. The lesson was that adults don't get to keep all the money they earn because they must pay taxes. Just as adults get police and fire protection and roads to drive on from their taxes, the children got a place to live, meals, and vacations from their "taxes."

When the children's dog got sick, they had to use part of their savings to help pay the veterinarian's bill. They learned what savings were for and how they could meet goals by saving ahead of time.

No child is too young to participate in the family budget. If your children are not part of your "budgeting board of directors," everyone gets cheated. They not only miss out on important lessons, but their feelings and wishes are not reflected in two strategic parts of family life: budgeting and buying decisions. However, the younger a child is, the shorter-term the goal must be to fit with a young child's short attention span and lack of patience.

## Parents

Your parents have lived longer and have survived more financial challenges than you have. Their individual and collective money personalities are important in terms of what kinds of help they can provide — and what kinds of help you *want* them to provide.

If your parents can handle requests for loans and advice in a businesslike manner (and if you'll respond with an equally businesslike attitude), you can ask for loans and advice. If they have the attitude that whoever pays gets to make the rules, they'll probably want more control and expect answers to more questions than you're willing to give them. If you're desperate for their help, one of the compromises you may have to live with is that you must live with *their* money personalities.

Just as you would negotiate the conditions of a new job before you accept it, you must negotiate the terms of your parents' involvement in your financial life before you agree to open that door.

## Friends

Friends have many of the same pluses and minuses that parents do, except you aren't required to keep them forever. You may think that you know your friends well, but when money enters the picture, personalities can clash.

Still, you may identify friends from whom you'd like advice on your finances. You can invite those friends into your financial circle based on your ability to work with the strengths and weaknesses of each person's money personality.

One of the benefits of friends' involvement in helping you reach your goals is that you can restrict them to just one area of your financial decision-making. If a friend gives you a loan, draw up a written agreement on the amount of the loan, when it is to be repaid, and how much interest is to be paid. If your friend suddenly decides that the loan gives him or her permission to tell you how to run your business or your life, remind your "friend" of the contract.

## Professional and free services

Professional sources can help you gather information, set goals, set priorities, or stay on your financial path. You can use these sources from the start, use them once in a while, or even discard them from your financial life once their purpose has been served.

*Accountants* do much more than fill out tax returns. They can help you set goals, remind you of factors that you have forgotten or ignored, use their backgrounds with a variety of people's problems and solutions to help you pick the best of both, start you on a good financial plan no matter what your age or income, help you revise your plans and goals as you get older, and — the part you'll probably enjoy the most — help you reduce the taxes you pay.

Depending on the accountant, you may also be able to get information about estate planning, insurance practices, housing, healthcare, and scholarships.

Your employer, union, or trade organization may have an *EAP (Employee Assistance Program).* The services that an EAP offers vary from provider to provider. Some EAPs offer budgeting, savings, tax, and estate planning services, either individually or in groups. They may also offer substance abuse help, family or individual counseling, workshops on buying and maintaining a home, and credit counseling. Whatever the topic, if you need information about it and don't pay for it, you've eliminated that budget expense while still learning what you need to know.

*Churches, temples, community groups, libraries, schools, alumni groups, financial institutions, credit bureaus, and associations such as Masons, Eastern Star, and Rotary* may offer budgeting and savings programs, either for free or at a low cost. Look in local newspapers and newsletters for ads announcing such programs. Your local library or social service agency may also keep track of such listings.

The program offerings from these groups may also include

- Avoiding repair costs through regular maintenance
- Building (or rebuilding) a good credit rating
- Buying the right amount of insurance for you
- Evaluating banking services
- Handling credit wisely
- Avoiding the hidden costs of holiday shopping
- Learning about programs that help pay for education, healthcare, housing, and utilities
- Purchasing your first home
- Surviving a layoff or divorce

## Dealing with Emergency Expenses

Unexpected expenses can severely disrupt your financial status. The three situations that usually get people in financial trouble are healthcare emergencies, expensive appliances that wear out, and vehicle repair and replacement.

Those expenses are the reason you have an emergency expense fund. (If you don't, go back to Chapter 3 and revise your budget!) If your fund isn't large enough, however, you can take short-term actions to avoid ending up in a spiral of debt:

- If your income is low, ask the local government or social services agency if low- or no-interest loans are available for these types of emergencies. Religious organizations may also have such funds.

- Ask your credit card companies and other creditors to let you skip a payment without penalty. They'll still add in an interest charge, which raises your total debt, but this tactic frees up immediate money so that you can take care of the emergency.

- Pawn some possessions. Pawning is really a secured loan — you get cash in exchange for an item of value. If you pay back the loan (with interest, of course) by the deadline, you can retrieve your item.

- If you have a medical emergency, ask your healthcare provider about available services that would offset expenses for you, such as free or low-cost housing and meals while your loved one is in the hospital.

- If your problem is with your car and you have a good relationship with a garage, try to negotiate a time-payment plan at low or no interest (rather than the higher rate that you would pay on a credit card).

- Take out a home-equity loan or second mortgage. These are not the best choices, however, because the rate of interest on them tends to be high. Also, read the fine print. On some of those loans, you could lose your house if you miss one loan payment. Make sure, too, that you have the right to pay the loan off early to cut the interest expense.

- If you belong to a social or service organization, find out whether it has a formal or informal system for helping members.

Be creative. This is another situation in which knowing the financial (and other) personalities of your family members and friends helps. Either the boldest family member or friend, or the one with the strongest "saver" personality, will be the best negotiator for these perks.

Paying for an emergency by credit card may get you in debt at a high interest rate. If you *must* use a credit card, be sure to choose the one with the lowest interest rate. Now may be the time to take advantage of a low-introductory-rate card that has been offered to you — but do so *only* if you can pay off the balance before the introductory rate expires, or if the regular rate is reasonable.

## If at First You Don't Succeed . . .

Popular knowledge says that cultivating a new habit takes 21 days. Doing something every day can change your life in three short weeks. Some financial habits are cultivated daily — packing lunches versus eating out, taking a taxi versus taking the bus, going to a movie versus watching television, listening to the radio versus buying a new CD, and so on. You can acquire good habits in these categories. Other financial matters — such as furniture and appliance shopping, choosing investment instruments, and so on — aren't things that you do every day, so learning new habits may take a little longer.

The Greek philosopher Aristotle said, "We are what we repeatedly do. Excellence is not an act, but a habit." You've already taken the time and trouble to gather information, learn new techniques, learn how to find help and new information, and set a budget and priorities. You wouldn't have pursued your goals with this amount of effort if you were going to give up at the first disappointment.

People make strange choices sometimes. Instead of giving ourselves credit for what we *have accomplished*, we worry about what we *still lack*. Don't fall into this pit of disappointment! As you review your budget, take time to savor how far you've come, and then pick which habit you want to tackle next and concentrate on it.

# CHAPTER 5
# REDUCING EXPENSES AND INCREASING YOUR INCOME

## IN THIS CHAPTER

- Analyzing how you currently spend your money
- Cutting your expenses
- Learning to make efficient financial choices
- Determining whether you need to make more money

Reducing your expenses may sound like a negative experience. Think of all the things you'll have to do without! When you finish this chapter, however, you'll feel the delight of having your spending under control. An added bonus is the disappearance of stress from not knowing how you're going to pay your bills and plan for your future. Because you'll have made spending decisions before you even leave your home, and because you'll know that sticking to those decisions will help you meet your goals, you won't spend time and energy on every spending decision.

If your best planning still finds "more month than money," the solution is to increase your income. Like you never thought of that, right? The difference is that in the past, your "plan" consisted of dreaming "if only I made more money." Here, you'll learn how to figure the amount you need, determine whether your need is short-term or long-term, and figure out exactly where you can find your personal pot of gold.

# Finding Alternatives to Spending

In Chapters 1 and 2, you gathered information about your spending habits from bank and credit card statements and your spending diary. Then you categorized your spending and figured out how much you spend by the day of the week. Now that you know where you're spending your money, when, and on what, you have all the information you need to reprioritize your spending.

Even when you purchase necessities, you can make bad decisions. For example, if you know that store brands of groceries are just as tasty as national brands and cost much less, but you continue to buy national brands, you aren't making good financial decisions. You can also make inefficient decisions by not identifying the true purpose of a purchase. You may want to buy a new outfit for a special occasion, so you ask the store clerk for such an outfit. But if you realize that your real purpose is to have something dressy to wear, you can pick something more versatile that you can wear to a wider variety of events.

**Tip**

As you categorize your spending, you can change your categories or even add and subtract categories. Remember that your system shouldn't frustrate you to the point that you stop making efforts to control your spending. Your financial health is important, so make it easy.

## Buy, rent, borrow, or co-own?

When the lawn is as high as an elephant's eye, do you go out and buy a lawn mower? Doing so would seem logical . . . except that your lawn takes only half an hour to mow — once a week, maximum.

Does your neighbor have the hugest, most magnificent maple tree in the state — with piles of autumn leaves in the yard to go with it? Raking all those leaves is a big job — for 1 month out of 12.

Earlier in this book, you started a list of everything you own. Expand that list by adding things that you forgot and then writing down what each item cost and how often you use it. Until you decided to get control of your spending, you probably thought that you needed each of these things because you actually use it. Listing how much it costs and how often you use it gives you a whole new perspective.

Remember that the cost of insuring, maintaining, and storing rarely used items is an ongoing expense, even on appliances that are paid for. Make sure to factor these costs into your list.

For each item that you own but rarely use, you have five choices:

- Keep it and use it until it wears out.

- Sell shares in the appliance to friends and neighbors who also have only intermittent need of the item.

- Sell the item and then rent or borrow a replacement only when you have a need for it.

- Sell the item and then pay someone to perform that chore with his or her own equipment.

- Find a lower-cost alternative to the item you need.

After picking one of these five choices, put a new cost on each item in your list. How much money could you free up by renting, borrowing, or co-owning?

Now that you have this information, how will you use it? The five choices tell you not only what to do with your current appliances, but also how to handle future needs. For example, when the leaf blower can't huff and puff anymore, you have five choices:

■  Replace it.

■  Rent a leaf blower only when the leaves come tumbling down.

■  Find friends and neighbors who have the same need, pool your money to purchase a new leaf blower, and take turns using it.

■  Make arrangements to borrow someone else's leaf blower when the need arises.

■  Use a rake.

Whether you're renting, borrowing, or co-owning, make sure that your "partners" share your attitude on maintenance, cleanup, storage, and general care of tools and appliances.

## Spend or barter?

With the proper incentive, anyone can make a deal. You may say that you don't know how to barter, but return for a minute to your childhood, and you'll see that you've always had the skill. Remember the words, "But Mom, if you buy me this toy, I'll eat all my vegetables for a week"?

In the grownup world, barter *is* negotiating. Maybe you want your washing machine fixed, your lawn mowed, or your gutters cleaned out. All you need to do is find something that you can do for someone else in return for the service you need.

Think about the things you can do that other people want done for them. Make a list of all the skills you use at work or in pursuing your hobbies — accessing the Internet, filling out tax returns, hanging wallpaper, taking photographs, and so on. Remember that personal skills (for example, closet reorganizing) and thinking skills (for example, planning a vacation) are tradable, too.

Using a fresh piece of paper (or a new word processing file), start a list of *all* your skills. Keep this list with you. As you go about your life, you'll think of more and more skills to add to this list. You may want to divide the list into things you're willing to do, things you'll do if you have to, and things you don't ever want to do again.

Consider bartering clubs, which may facilitate this part of your money management. To find a bartering club, look in your local Yellow Pages, ask a librarian, or check with neighborhood organizations, trade associations, service organizations, alumni associations, and churches.

Every club has its own rules, but, like any other organization, someone has to pay the organization's costs. If you're interested in joining a bartering club, you need to know the following information:

■ Is there a fee to join? An annual fee?

■ What fees are assessed on barters?

■ Who belongs now? (Get a list to make sure that the members live close enough to you and match the sorts of trades you'll want to make.)

■ Are the club membership and services growing or shrinking?

■ How long has the club been in existence?

■ Can you drop your membership whenever you want, as long as you "pay" whatever outstanding "debt" is in your account?

Find out as much as you can about a club before you join. If other members aren't reliable, are so fussy that they'll always complain about your contributions, or live so far away that they can't fulfill your needs, don't join.

# Making Over Your Lifestyle

Giving your lifestyle a makeover is *not* the same as lowering your standard of living or depriving yourself. In fact, it can be quite the opposite. The emphasis here is on *style*. As the preceding sections on sharing and bartering demonstrate, a lifestyle makeover involves an attitude shift that will help you get the most for your dollar. The following sections can help you reach your financial goals and at the same time improve the *style* in your life.

## Use coupons rather than pay full price

The art of saving money by using coupons has become a consumer industry in itself. Whether you've never used coupons or you use them regularly and want to get more from your efforts, the tips in this section can help you meet your goals.

"Couponing" is a skill for which reading carefully really pays off. First, you have to find coupons. Check newspapers and newspaper inserts, the telephone book, the packaging of items you've already bought, the back of your supermarket receipts, and coupon trade boxes inside stores, to name a few sources. Then you must remember to use the coupons you clip. Make sure to take them with you when you shop!

You can get more than face value for your coupons by shopping at stores that "double," or give you twice what the coupon is worth.

Don't buy something just because you have a coupon for it. If you won't use the product for a while, you have to store it; if it's something you don't like, you'll never use it.

## Live like a Rockefeller on a Rockette's salary

Organizations to which you belong can come to your aid with special deals that help you live the life you want but spend less for it. For example, a credit union might coordinate a special one-day sale of used cars for its members. If you wanted a nicer car, you could purchase one for less money than you thought you'd have to spend.

Other groups, such as unions, fraternal and alumni organizations, and public service groups (like the Lions Club, Rotary, or Soroptimist) offer similar deals to their members. Because these organizations buy in bulk, they often get lower rates and can pass the savings along to you.

If you're planning a car trip and a gasoline credit card travel club offers hotel discounts, this may be the time to obtain that card. If you have trouble with overspending on credit cards, cut up the credit card and mail it back to the company with a note to cancel your account as soon as the trip is over.

## Remember that you don't have to spend a lot to have fun

When you first determined to get your financial house in order, you probably thought that entertainment was going to go by the wayside. Even with cable, television is a pretty poor long-term amusement. Luckily, you have many other options.

If theater, opera, live music, and so on are your passion, you can enjoy them without breaking open the piggy bank. Many of these events use volunteer ushers. If you usher, you attend for free. The downside is that you may have to see the same play ten times — and you can't walk out on a stinker. In the long run, however, you'll have a good time for only the price of transportation or parking.

Some travel agencies sell off cruises and other deals at very good prices to people who can fill vacancies at the last minute. You can buy into these deals at 50 percent or less of the listed price.

Sometimes you have to become a member of a travel club in order to be notified of an opening. Make sure that you will use or save enough to make the membership fees worthwhile.

## Spend less and enjoy life more

Look for your own opportunities to reduce your expenses without reducing your quality of life. Instead of always looking to your wallet to pay for entertainment, use the creative skills that you've been developing. Knowledgeable, reliable people are in demand everywhere.

- Do you live near a school that needs monitors to take students to see matinees? Volunteer for the job.

- If you can't devote the time to be a regular usher at the theater, offer a skill or time in trade for attending a dress rehearsal.

- If you like sports, find out what personnel are needed to put on an event. Could you hold the measuring chains at football games? Does a track meet need a timer?

- Do you like music? Offer to be a music page turner for rehearsal sessions.

## Living on Less

If you went to the store to buy one size and brand of bread and could pay $2.00 or $2.50 for it, which would you choose? This sounds like a dumb question, yet people make the wrong decision every day.

Here are some ways to live on less without sacrificing quality of life:

■   Shop at discount stores instead of convenience stores and buy the same items for less. Head to the library for a local or area-wide directory of discount and outlet stores.

■   Take your lunch instead of buying it; you'll eat a healthier lunch and save money, too.

■   Negotiate with your employer to work at home. By doing so, you can save restaurant, travel, car wear and tear, and clothing expenses.

Warning

Negotiate who is going to pay for the equipment, telephone lines, and other expenses. If those expenses are your responsibility, you may be spending instead of saving money.

■   Understand your real goal before you make a purchase. If you want to lose weight, for example, you can do so for free by walking in the park or by taking advantage of the company gym. Either one is cheaper than signing a contract at a health club.

■   A used car is "new" to you. You not only pay less, but the insurance costs are less than on a new car, depreciation is slower, and you don't have to dread that first ding in the door.

■   *Always* use a shopping list. Just as the lines on the highway keep you driving in the lane, a shopping list keeps you from giving in to temptation. Even if you decide to purchase something that's not on your list, you will have considered and weighed the purchase.

## Hanging onto Your "Found" Money

The fastest way to undo all your hard work is to think of your money as a tradeoff between spending on one item and spending on another. Yes, you can take advantage of the savings that come from buying in larger quantities — *if* you've figured for waste, storage costs, and the other possible expenses of having a large quantity of one item on hand.

If you release yourself from always worrying about money by reducing your expenses, you may feel "rich" because you at last have cash in your pocket. That "found" money should go first toward debt reduction (which Chapter 6 discusses in depth). Once you're out of debt, don't look for places to spend the newly released money; you've already promised that money to your savings plan (see Chapter 7).

Does paying off debts and then putting money toward savings mean that you don't get to enjoy the fruits of your labor? Of course not. You get to enjoy being free from worry, seeing your debts disappear, and watching your savings grow.

While you're paying off debts and starting a savings program with your "found" money, don't even *think* about the credit available on your credit cards. Using that credit means more debt, which is exactly what you *don't* want.

## Earning Additional Income

If all your money-saving, coupon-cutting, and planning still leave you short of your goals, look for ways to earn more income. Getting a raise would be nice — and it's even possible! Contact trade associations, your alumni association, and unions and do research at the library or on the Internet to find out what others doing your job are making. If you find that your wage is lower than average, take your research to your boss and ask for a raise.

Tip

Also, in the same way that you took inventory of your spending and your belongings, take an inventory of your skills. Look for skills that you use at work but that maybe aren't appreciated by your boss and aren't being recognized in your paycheck. Bosses don't have to think about what's going right . . . so they don't! You need to remind your boss about your accomplishments. If you can prove that you're underpaid, negotiate a raise.

Do you have hobbies that can earn you extra money? For example, if you know how to work with wood, you can sell the furniture that you build or help people build things for a fee. You may have to do a little research to see how much you should charge customers, but hobbies still are a good source of income that's a pleasure to earn.

You not only need to survey your knowledge and skills to see where you might earn extra income, but you also must decide how much you want to earn and what it will cost you to do so. Remember to calculate material and tool expenditures as well as time expenditures. Will you recoup your investment? Will you have enough income to write off those expenditures on your income taxes as business expenses? Will you have to eat more meals in restaurants? Will your transportation costs go up? Do you want to spend more time doing what you do at your regular job, or something else entirely?

Once you've decided what you want to do and set an hourly income goal, form a plan that fits your needs.

- **Short-term need:** If you want to do extra work only long enough to pay off your credit card or other debt, you may want to look for seasonal work or register with a temporary agency. Because you won't be working extra for a long time (you get to define *long*), you'll probably have the energy to work longer hours, work more days per week, commute a little farther, and so on.

■ **Mid-term need:** If you need the extra income for a longer period, such as while your child grows up, you don't want to commit yourself to so many hours, so much travel, or so many days per week that you don't have a life. That's a quick way to burn out. Not only will you fail to reach your goals, but you'll be discouraged. Consider trading some income for cutting back on your lifestyle.

■ **Long-term need:** To earn extra income for a long-term need, such as retirement, consider the same options that you did for a mid-term need. Recognize that the decisions you make will affect your lifestyle for a longer time.

If you're going to be forced to spend more time at work, have more commuting costs, have wasted "dead" time (blocks of time between jobs that are long enough to be annoying but short enough that you can't really use them for naps, grocery shopping, or whatever), it may be time to consider cutting back on your lifestyle. Moving to less expensive housing, sharing housing, purchasing items on sale, bartering more aggressively, and so on will allow you to make more life-enhancing decisions sooner.

# CHAPTER 6

# TACKLING YOUR DEBT

## IN THIS CHAPTER

- Totaling your debt
- Reviewing your spending plan to avoid adding to your debt
- Repaying your debts
- Deciding whether you need to consolidate your debts

By now (that is, if you've read Chapters 1 through 5), you must be convinced that a systematic plan is the secret to getting a handle on your finances. Although the choices you'll make about handling your debt may be somewhat complicated, you have all the skills and knowledge that you need to create an effective debt-repayment plan. This chapter shows you how to apply those skills and knowledge.

## Figuring Out How Much You Owe

To find out how much you owe, the first step is to do a personal debt survey. This survey is a little easier than a budget survey because you need only your latest statement from each debt. Gather the following documents:

- Coupon book for your mortgage payments
- Coupon book(s) for your automobile payments
- Credit card statements
- Department store card statements

- Loan statements (If you haven't started paying back a loan yet, call the lender and ask for the total amount due.)

- Paperwork for private loans from relatives and friends (Keep good records so that no dispute occurs.)

On a piece of paper, or by using your budgeting software or a spreadsheet program, create a table like Table 6-1. The information you gathered in Chapter 2 by surveying your checkbook records will help you do so quickly and completely.

Tip

To see how much your debt is costing you, call each lender and ask how much you paid in interest last year. Record those amounts in your debt register. Remember that you received *no* benefit from all that money you paid in interest.

### Table 6-1:  My Debt Register

| Account | Total Amount Due | Monthly Payment | Total Interest Paid Last Year | Interest Rate |
|---------|------------------|-----------------|-------------------------------|---------------|
| VISA | $4,568 | $115 | $639 | 12.9% |
| MasterCard | $2,372 | $86 | $481 | 15.9% |
| Home Repairs, Inc. | $1,423 | $67 | $314 | 18.5% |
| Car payment | $15,268 | $236 | $1,162 | 7.1% |
| Mortgage | $117,469 | $916 | $8,437 | 6.7% |

# Reducing Your Consumer Debt

*Consumer debt* is any money you owe *except* your mortgage. It includes credit card and loan debts. Most financial planners warn that if your consumer debt is more than 20 percent of your monthly net income, you're probably going to be unable to pay your monthly obligations. In your debt register, is the total of your monthly payments, minus your mortgage payment, below 20 percent of your net income? Even if it is, don't feel good just yet. Your long-term goal is to pay off all your consumer debt every month so that you don't pay interest to anyone.

Many banks charge an annual fee on their credit cards if you pay off your monthly invoices so that you don't pay any interest. Credit unions are owned by their members, so they don't tend to have such hidden costs.

## Pay off high-interest-rate credit cards first

Getting the balance on your credit cards down to $0 feels good. Because it seems to be a giant step toward the goal of having no consumer debt, many debtors pay extra money on their lowest-balance cards. That is *not* the way to speed up the reduction of your debt, however. Even if you make no new purchases on your highest-interest cards, you end up paying interest on the interest that you already were charged! How does that happen? Your original debt *plus* the interest amount becomes the new amount on which next month's interest cost is based.

The best payoff system is two-part: First, if you can, move balances from high-interest cards to low-interest cards. Then pay the minimum due on your low-interest cards and pay as much as possible on your high-interest cards. By paying off your high-interest-rate cards first, you save the most money.

Tables 6-2 and 6-3 offer a comparison of how the interest rate affects your ability to pay off your debt. In this example, I used *simple interest* (computed monthly as a flat rate). Credit card companies and other credit debt holders often compute interest daily — in which case the effects of paying interest on interest are even more devastating!

**Table 6-2:    Your Debt Cost at 11.9 Percent Annual Interest**

| Month | Balance | Yearly Interest Rate X 12 | Interest Debt This Month | New Balance | Payment |
|---|---|---|---|---|---|
| 1 | $5,000.00 | 0.991666% | $49.58 | 5,049.58 | 150.00 |
| 2 | $4,899.58 | 0.991666% | $48.58 | 4,948.16 | 150.00 |
| 3 | $4,798.16 | 0.991666% | $47.58 | 4,845.74 | 150.00 |
| 4 | $4,695.74 | 0.991666% | $46.57 | 4,742.31 | 150.00 |
| 5 | $4,592.31 | 0.991666% | $45.54 | 4,637.85 | 150.00 |
| 6 | $4,487.85 | 0.991666% | $44.50 | 4,532.35 | 150.00 |

Total interest paid in six months:   $282.35

Total of payments for six months:   $467.65

Percent of payoff that is interest:   50

**Table 6-3:    Your Debt Cost at 8.9 Percent Annual Interest**

| Month | Balance | Yearly Interest Rate X 12 | Interest Debt This Month | New Balance | Payment |
|---|---|---|---|---|---|
| 1 | $5,000.00 | 0.741666% | $37.08 | 5,037.08 | 150.00 |
| 2 | $4,887.08 | 0.741666% | $36.25 | 4,923.33 | 150.00 |
| 3 | $4,773.33 | 0.741666% | $35.40 | 4,808.73 | 150.00 |

| Month | Balance | Yearly Interest Rate X 12 | Current Interest Debt | New Balance | Payment |
|---|---|---|---|---|---|
| 4 | $4,658.73 | 0.741666% | $34.55 | 4,693.28 | 150.00 |
| 5 | $4,543.28 | 0.741666% | $33.70 | 4,576.98 | 150.00 |
| 6 | $4,426.98 | 0.741666% | $32.83 | 4,459.81 | 150.00 |

Total interest paid in six months: $209.81

Total of payments for six months: $690.19

Percent of payoff that is interest: 30

Table 6-3 shows that in just six months, you save $72.54 by paying a 3 percent lower annual interest rate. Your balance due at the lower rate is $222.54 less than at the higher rate. From this example, you can see how paying off your higher-rate cards first saves you money, gets you out of debt faster, and helps you pay less interest.

Tip

An adage says that if you owe enough money, your creditors become your partners. Call your credit card companies or the holders of your loans to ask for help in rescheduling your payments. Many companies help finance credit counseling services to help their customers (and themselves) by keeping you from filing bankruptcy. You can also contact your local Better Business Bureau for a list of its credit counselor members. These services charge a nominal fee that is often shared by your creditors. You can also look in the Yellow Pages under "Credit Counselors."

You can also get help from the nonprofit National Foundation for Consumer Credit Counseling. For help in English, call 800-388-2227; for help in Spanish, call 800-682-9832. You can also contact the foundation on the Internet at www.nfic.org to get information or to find a service near you.

*Do not* use credit repair services that you see advertised on telephone poles and subway walls. They can't do anything that you can't either do yourself or use a legitimate credit-counseling service to do for you. On top of that, these fly-by-night firms charge for their "service" — money that you could have used to pay down your debt. Legitimate counselors do not promise "credit repair," because the only way to earn a good credit rating is to pay your bills on time.

## Using department store credit cards wisely — or not at all

As with other credit cards, there's a good way and a bad way to use department store credit cards. First, be aware that these cards tend to charge high interest rates. That doesn't mean that you shouldn't use them at all; just use them wisely and pay the balance each month. Also be aware that holding such cards means that the stores will bombard you with mailings. You learn about sales, but you may be tempted to buy things that you don't need.

As Chapter 5 advises, always shop with a list. Because you'll have taken an inventory of everything in your home and will keep that list up to date, you'll know whether you really need that beautiful new coat on the cover of the latest store mailer.

If you're trying to rebuild your credit, department store cards can be a good way to do so. They're relatively easy to get — if your credit rating isn't good, you just get a low maximum. And these cards don't charge annual fees. The combination gives you a chance to charge carefully, pay religiously, and improve your credit history.

Department store card balances can sneak up on you. Along with high interest rates, these cards often have a low minimum payment due. As you learned earlier in this chapter, the longer you stretch out paying off the balance, the more interest you pay. And as Tables 6-2 and 6-3 demonstrate, higher interest rates make a big difference in a short time in the amount you have to pay back.

### Stop using your credit cards

All habits can be a challenge to break. The real problem with breaking spending habits is that it's more like controlling food than controlling tobacco. As hard as it may be, you can avoid tobacco. But you have to eat, and you have to spend money. So the real secret is control, not abstinence.

Keep your goals in mind. Use your written budget, financial plan, and spending diary to keep yourself on track. Once you enjoy the lack of stress from overspending, see yourself working toward your goals, and get to enjoy reaching personal as well as financial objectives, you'll make better choices.

One good thing about using credit cards is the statements. They give you information about your spending habits in an easily accessible form. If you can resist overspending and unplanned spending, you can use your credit cards again. Because your new way of handling credit cards will look good on your credit report, you'll be able to get lower-interest cards, lower-rate loans, and a lower-rate mortgage. Your good financial reputation will give you leverage to negotiate other financial deals.

## Paying Back Your Loans

You handle loans like you handle credit card debt: You prioritize which loans to pay first, based on their rates. (The exception is mortgages, which you can read about later in this chapter.) And you want to avoid new debt.

If you run into a rough patch financially, call your lenders and make deals for deferring payments *before* your payments are late. But be very careful when you negotiate. The interest rate on some loans rises automatically if you're late or you defer payment(s). Negotiate to keep your interest rate the same!

When you've tallied six months or more of faithful payments, ask your creditors to lower your interest rates.

## Student and educational loans

If you're sorry now that you took out those student loans, you still have a lot to learn about personal finance. Student loans are an investment in your future. Graduating from college is still a good investment, even after you pay off your loans. Table 6-4 shows the results of a 1993 Census Bureau release that calculated lifetime earnings according to educational level.

**Table 6-4:    U.S. Lifetime Earnings by Educational Level**

| High School | Bachelor's Degree | Master's Degree | Professional Degree |
|---|---|---|---|
| $821,000 | $1,421,000 | $1,619,000 | $3,000,000+ |

And the gap is widening. So take a deep breath, roll up your sleeves, and put the loan payback into your budget.

If your only experience with timed payments is with car payments, you may think that your only repayment option is to pay equal amounts each month until your debt is paid. These are called *standard repayments*. The good news is that standard repayments are predictable. The bad news is that you're making payments when you're just out of school, trying to set up a household, buy a professional wardrobe, and start a new life. So perhaps another repayment plan would suit your life better.

Consider asking your lender for graduated payments. When you first get out of school and have high expenses and not-so-high income, making lower payments is easier. As you progress in your career, with presumably high pay, your payments also increase.

Although this plan extends your payments and you pay more in interest, it also arranges for you to match higher payments with higher income. As an added bonus, your good payment record enhances your overall credit rating. A good credit rating means that you'll be able to qualify for credit cards, mortgages, and other loans at lower interest rates than can people who have bad credit records.

Another possibility is a payment schedule based on your income. Student loans are guaranteed by the government agency Sallie Mae (Student Loan Marketing Association). This guarantee gives you the option of paying between 4 and 25 percent of your gross monthly income on your loan. Again, you'll pay more in interest over the length of the loan than you would with a standard repayment plan. But if you expect to start your career at a fairly low salary with the promise of salary growth, an income-based plan can help you keep your payments proportionate to your salary and your credit rating good.

When paying down your debt, your student loan should probably be last on your list. Because the interest rate is low and interest is added only once a month, this is probably your lowest-cost loan.

The best news is that you don't have to choose a payment plan and stay with it. If your financial picture changes, you can negotiate a new plan. If your finances change drastically — for example, if you become ill or unemployed — you may even be able to defer some payments. Interest will continue accruing, but you should be able to negotiate waiving of late payment penalties.

Your best negotiating position is when you contact the lender, not when you get behind in your payments and the lender contacts you. Again, because student loans tend to cost the least, they should be your first choice for deferred payment.

Keeping track of your ability to pay and making adjustments to your payment plan *before* you have financial problems is the way use your education debt to build a good credit report.

## Car loans

You probably need a car for transportation. Before you think about how much you can afford, you need to identify your needs (versus your desires) so that you can make good financial decisions and not bow to sales pressure. With a needs list in place, you can resist the sales pressure when you see all the goodies available.

Before buying something from the "goodies list," look at the *overall* cost, not the "little bit more" that it costs each month to have monogrammed floor mats (or whatever).

Shop around for loan rates before you go car shopping. Then you can focus your energies on one item at a time: first the loan, and then the car. When you secure the loan, make sure that there is no prepayment penalty. Read your dealership or lender contract carefully to avoid additional fees and penalties. Also, make sure to tell the lender that all excess payments are to be applied to the principal portion of the loan so that your interest payments decrease even more with each payment.

When you're deciding how to pay down your debts, evaluate the interest rate and compounding policy (the total *cost* of the loan). Once you have this information, you can compare it to your other debts to prioritize loan repayments.

## Mortgages

Your housing costs are part of your short-term, mid-term, and long-term goals in Chapter 1. But a budget is a living, changing thing. To meet your current goals, you may want to update your strategies.

If loan rates have fallen since you financed your home, now may be the time to renegotiate or refinance. Remember that there are costs associated with this process, such as application fees, points, and so on. Will you be in the home long enough to recoup that money and save over time from the lower interest rate? If not, refinancing isn't for you.

If you do refinance, be careful about the "small" things that can add big costs, just like you did when you first got a loan. Fees, penalties, closing costs, prepayment penalties, and so forth can wipe out your "savings" from refinancing very quickly. If you take a longer-term loan than you need, the interest rate may be lower than that on your current loan, but higher than the rate you would get on a shorter-term loan now. Try to refinance for the time it would take to pay off your current mortgage. Or use the lower interest rate to pay your current amount, but for a shorter time.

Remember

If you choose to pay more than you owe in any month, write a separate check and clearly mark it "for principal only." If you don't specify, the bank will pay itself first — that is, apply the money to interest instead of principal.

In general, your mortgage is the last debt you want to prepay. It probably has a lower interest rate than any other debt on your plate. Additionally, you can deduct mortgage interest from your federal taxable income. In some states, mortgage interest payments are deductible on state income tax returns as well.

# Consolidating Your Bills as a Next-to-Last Resort

If you created your own debt register like the one in Table 6-1, you can see how much you must pay every month just to pay the minimums on your credit cards and loans. Add your mortgage or rent payment and monthly living expenses, and the total can be overwhelming.

If you can't meet your monthly obligations, no matter how well you budget or how much you can expect to earn from you job(s), you may need a consolidation loan. For this type of loan, the lender pays off all the obligations that you decide to put under the plan. That total is the amount of your loan. You then pay one manageable bill to the lender every month.

Sounds great, doesn't it? The problem is that the interest rate on the consolidation loan is probably as high as that on your *highest* previous debt, and the term is probably longer than that on your *longest* previous debt. Therefore, the cost to you over the term of the loan is much higher than the cost of paying off your debts under their original terms.

Warning

If your consolidation loan is secured by your home — a home equity loan — you can lose your home if you can't make your payments. Companies specialize in making these types of loans so that they can take possession of the property at the first missed payment. Unlike mortgage lenders that try to help borrowers keep their homes, the purpose of "shark" lenders is to profit by taking over property for as little investment as possible.

A consolidation loan looks bad on your credit record. The result may be that in the future, you'll have to borrow at a higher interest rate than if you had paid the debts without consolidating. But a consolidation loan looks a lot better than a default or bankruptcy!

## Filing Bankruptcy as a Last Resort

*Bankruptcy* is the legal cancellation of your debts when you're unable to repay them. Bankruptcy is *not* wiping the slate clean. Although it relieves you of the responsibility for paying past debts, it stays on your credit report for up to ten years, which makes it hard to get credit. Also, you'll pay more — in interest rates, annual fees, application fees, and whatever else lenders can think of — for the credit you can get.

You can get bankruptcy kits at bookstores. Doing so takes time and concentration, but you can fill out the legal papers yourself. If you want to have your papers checked (or you don't even want to attempt an admittedly complicated process), an accountant can do a good job for you at a much lower cost than a lawyer. When you go for help, ask your professional to offer an alternative to bankruptcy — you'll already have gathered the information needed to see whether you can pay off your debts in some way.

Never use a professional whose sole purpose is to file bankruptcy as opposed to offering good financial advice.

Your papers must be filed with the federal district court for the area in which you live. A court-appointed trustee reviews your application for bankruptcy and recommends to the court whether it should be approved. If your application is not approved, you receive no refund on the fees paid to the court, and you must find a reliable credit counselor to plan a repayment schedule. This is yet another reason to have a professional prepare or review your bankruptcy papers with an eye toward avoiding having to file them at all.

## CHAPTER 7
# PUTTING MONEY AWAY FOR THE FUTURE

## IN THIS CHAPTER

- Identifying your attitude toward risk
- Looking at the available savings and investing instruments
- Making decisions based on the length of time to your goal
- Tracking the performance of your investments

While creating a budget, you learn the multiple benefits of paying off your debts. Paying off debts not only erases the debts themselves but also enables you to stop wasting money by paying interest and releases funds for investing. You want to make the most of those "found" dollars and invest them wisely.

This chapter shows you how to determine which types of savings and investment vehicles will work for you and your goals. It also shows you how to keep track of the investments in which you decide to put your money.

## Identifying Your Saving and Investing Personality

Like a money personality (discussed in Chapter 2), you have a personality that impacts how you go about pursuing savings and investment goals. Your saving and investing personality reflects how much risk you're willing to take for higher returns.

Risk tolerance is equivalent to an exerciser's tolerance of pain. If you don't believe in pain, you have a *low* risk tolerance — you're willing to accept low interest rates in return for not worrying about your investments. If you think that you probably need to have a muscle twinge or two to see results, you have a *moderate* risk tolerance — you're willing to take some risk in pursuit of a higher return on investment. If you think that if you don't need medical care after your workout, you haven't really worked out, you have a *high* tolerance of risk — you're willing to take big risks in hopes that your investments will grow fast and furiously, and you also feel that you can rebuild your financial foundation if you lose a bundle.

Identify your savings/investment personality in the following list:

- **Low risk-taker:** Your primary concern is to conserve your money. People who can't afford to have their nest eggs shrink at all — such as retirees, widows and widowers, and novice and low-income savers — fall into this group.

  Low risk-takers depend on compounding interest for growth in their savings plans. Savings accounts, certificates of deposit, and other "sure" investments are in their portfolios. These folks can't (or think that they can't) take risks. Retirees no longer have paychecks coming in to make up losses. Novice investors can't afford to lose the modest nest eggs they have because they'll fall far behind in their investment plans if they have to build those nest eggs again.

  Worrying about the safety of your investments will not keep you up nights if you're a low risk-taker. However, during periods of economic growth, with stable prices but low interest rates, investors in this category can lose ground. Even the most committed low risk-takers must switch some funds to higher-yielding instruments so that inflation doesn't erode their buying power.

■ **Moderate risk-taker:** A moderate risk-taker is more daring than a low risk-taker but is still a conservative investor. Moderates are often in the midst of their income-earning years. Their goals include putting their children through college and planning for retirement. Keeping even with inflation will not enable them to reach these goals. On the other hand, moderates don't want to go for the "big kill" (really high returns) because that strategy is accompanied by high risk.

Moderates can take some risk because they're still in their income-earning years and, by changing their budgets, can make up some of the loss from an investment that has gone bad.

■ **High risk-taker:** High-risk investors look for large returns on their investments. Sometimes, people who are just starting their careers are high risk-takers because they don't have family responsibilities. Also, because they expect their incomes to increase, they have time to rebuild from a loss.

Other high-risk investors are speculators, who enjoy the thrill of hunting down that big return. Sometimes, speculators take the time to be extremely well informed about investments and feel sure of them. Other times, they just hope to get lucky.

Most people have parts of each personality. You may be a higher risk-taker when you know more about an investment, a low risk-taker when you're uninformed or thinking about protecting your core investment, and a moderate when you know a little and feel somewhat confident.

Just as you have some of each investment personality in you, your investment *portfolio* (the group of investments that you hold) needs to reflect some of each type of risk. This setup makes the most of your investment dollars and enables you to reach your goals in a manner that's comfortable for you.

This type of investment mixture is called a *balanced portfolio*. Here, *balanced* doesn't mean having the same amount in each risk category. Rather, you determine the amount to put in each risk category by taking into account your comfort level and your needs so that your portfolio works for you.

No one mixture of investments is best for everyone. For example, a low risk-taker needs to conserve capital. The goal is to ensure having a nest egg but to get some higher returns to at least balance the erosion of inflation. This person will probably want 50 percent of investments in low-risk investment, perhaps 30 percent in moderate-risk, and 20 percent in high-risk. This mix provides a "safe" base.

Someone who is even more fearful of losing his or her nest egg may invest even more conservatively. The investment in low-risk investments may be 60 percent, with 30 percent in moderate-risk and only 10 percent in high-risk.

Even low risk-takers can be daring within their own parameters, though. A "daredevil" might divide the portfolio with 40 percent in low-risk investments, 30 percent in moderate-risk, and 30 percent in high-risk.

## Understanding Different Savings and Investment Instruments

There's no one "right" savings or investment instrument for everyone, because the needs that shape your choices come together in a unique pattern. The following sections take a look at the most common instruments. (By the way, "savings and investment instruments" is just a high-tone way of saying "where you keep your money.")

## Savings and money market accounts

Savings accounts and money market accounts are good places to save for short-term goals, such as buying a new piece of furniture. Because withdrawing your funds from one of these accounts is easy, you can take advantage of special deals as they come up.

The main difference between a savings account and a money market account is that a savings account is offered by a bank, and a money market account is offered by a mutual fund company. If you want to put money in either type of account, look for the highest interest rate, but make sure that no off-setting fees apply, or that the cost of doing business with that institution doesn't eat up your interest — or even worse, your principal.

Banks may charge you a fee to keep a savings account with a low balance. If you keep a small sum in an account but the bank imposes a monthly, quarterly, or annual charge when your balance falls below a certain amount, then you may be better off keeping your money under your mattress.

Credit unions are a great way to avoid these types of fees. Credit unions are owned by their members, so they don't need to dream up hidden charges or nasty little policies to pick your pocket. You'll not only save on fees and charges, but the interest rates on credit union loans are lower as well. And the interest rates that credit unions pay on savings accounts are comparable to the rates that banks pay.

## Certificates of deposit

Certificates of deposit usually earn higher rates of interest than savings accounts do, but they don't charge fees like mutual funds and stock and bond investments (described later in this section). Unlike a savings account, you can't add to the deposit or withdraw money before the CD's maturity date without paying a penalty.

The good news with a CD is that you know exactly what to expect. When you purchase a CD, you agree to a certain return, unlike the fluctuating rate of a savings account. Obviously, you want to shop around for the highest rate.

Your CD is due at a stated period, which may be months or years. (The longer the term, the higher the rate of return.) When that date comes, you may reinvest or take your earnings. If you cash in your CD before its due date, you have to pay a penalty.

**Warning**

If you have a certificate of deposit or similar account that charges a penalty for taking out cash before a certain date, and you use this account to pay bills, you are, in effect, throwing money away. You lose the amount of the penalty and get nothing to show for it. It's like going out to dinner and paying for your meal, but not being allowed to eat it. If you need cash while you have money tied up in a CD, you may be better off taking out a loan by using the CD for security. You avoid the early-withdrawal penalty, which may be more than the cost of the loan.

## 401(k) and Keogh plans

Both of these plans are voluntary retirement savings plans. The difference between the two plans is that the employer funds a 401(k), and Keogh plans are for self-employed people.

These plans are great places to put your "future money" because you can use pretax dollars — you pay taxes when you withdraw funds in retirement. Also, 401(k) investments are often deducted from your paycheck automatically (after you request the deduction, of course!), so you won't be tempted to spend that money rather than put it away. You are allowed to put only a certain amount of your income in these types of funds, however, so look to other types of investments as well.

## Individual retirement accounts (IRAs)

Individual retirement accounts, or IRAs, are tax-sheltered accounts for retirement investing. You may invest up to $2,000 per year in an IRA. There are two types of IRAs; the type you choose depends on what you think your retirement taxable income will be.

■ **Traditional IRAs:** Contributions may be tax-deductible (depending on your income). Earnings are tax-deferred — that is, they're not taxed until you start making withdrawals.

■ **Roth IRAs:** These accounts are paid from pre-income tax funds, but withdrawals can be tax-free.

If you start withdrawing funds from either type of IRA before age 59½, you must pay a penalty.

## Mutual funds

A mutual fund pools your money with that of the other investors in the fund and then invests the money on behalf of all the investors. Mutual funds spread out the risk by investing in many companies, stocks, bonds, CDs, and other instruments.

The good thing about mutual funds is that they lower your risk. First, they're managed by professionals, who presumably are able to make wise investment choices. Second, they invest in a range of stocks, bonds, and other vehicles (known as *diversification*), which means that poor performance of some elements is offset by the good performance of others.

Warning

Mutual funds are not appropriate for an investment of less than two years because your return will not cover the fees that you pay.

Choosing a mutual fund may seem daunting, because thousands are available. You can narrow the possibilities by answering the following questions:

- What is your risk-tolerance factor? (See the section "Identifying Your Saving and Investing Personality," earlier in this chapter, if you need help answering this question.) Some funds are "safer," and some take bigger risks in hopes of higher returns.

- Do you want income from your investments, or do you want your earnings to be rolled over for further investment? Choose the appropriate type of account for your needs:

  A *dividends account* is for people who need income to live on.

  A *capital value account* is for people who are trying to maximize the size of their accounts by reinvesting their earnings.

- Do you want to invest in domestic, foreign, or mixed companies? Different funds specialize in different types of companies.

- Do you want to pay your management costs when you invest or when you withdraw from the fund?

As you narrow your choices, you'll think of other questions that will guide you to finding the right fund for you.

Tip

After you narrow down your list of prospective funds to a manageable number, investigate the fund manager's track record. The fund manager is the person who chooses the fund's investments, so you want to know that he or she has invested successfully in the past.

# Analyzing Which Instruments Are Best for You

In choosing a savings or investment instrument, you need to match your goals and your comfort level with three factors:

■ The interest rate earned

■ The time frame in which you want to reach your goal(s)

■ The fees, penalties, and other costs associated with the investment

Interest rates, also known as *rates of return* or *ROR,* are never confusing. When you're receiving interest, you want the highest rate you can get. If the interest is compounded, you want it to be compounded (or "rolled over") in the smallest time increments possible because that's how your money grows the fastest. Simple interest is the least desirable; continuous compounding is the most desirable.

The time frame is a little bit trickier. For short-term goals, such as a new car or a new baby, you want to be able to convert your investment into cash easily and in a short time. You miss the advantages of compounding interest, but you also miss the aggravation of inflating prices. You could invest in 6-month, 9-month, or 12-month certificates of deposit, for example. These investments will earn interest for you, and thus grow, while you wait for the date of your goal.

The longer you commit to an investment, the larger the guaranteed interest rate usually is. An investment of $1,000 in a 3-month CD may have an annual interest rate of 3.1 percent, whereas a 12-month CD purchased at the same time may have an annual interest rate of 5.5 percent.

For longer-term goals, you can afford a bit more fluctuation. Depending on your needs, you might choose a mutual fund or, if you're not comfortable with that level of risk, choose to put money in your company's 401(k) program. Like any other investment, however, you need to watch the changes that affect your investment so that you reach your goals.

When choosing savings and investment instruments, carefully read the information about fees. Doing so is even more crucial when you're just starting out. If a fund has a fixed fee of $50 and you're investing $100,000, the fee is a small price to pay for doing business with that fund (0.05 percent). If you're investing only $1,000, however, $50 is a substantial bite out of your investable dollars (5 percent).

Never make assumptions about the terms of any of your savings or investment instruments. If changes are made to one of your instruments, read the new terms and then keep the notices on file.

## Investing Your Money: The Earlier the Better

Learning about compounding shows you the benefits of starting a savings and investment plan early. Because you earn interest now on the interest already earned, your income multiplies faster. Compounded interest is one of the reasons that putting yourself on a tight budget early in your income-earning years pays off later.

Although the amount that you regularly add to your investment fund may decrease as you pay for a house, raise children, seek more education, care for your elderly parents, and so on, the money that you put in earlier is still growing. Table 7-1 shows the consequences of your decision of when to start saving and investing.

**Table 7-1:    The Timing of Your Investment Influences Your Return**

| Mary Anne | | | | Karl | | | |
| --- | --- | --- | --- | --- | --- | --- | --- |
| Age | Years | Contributions | End-of-Year Value | Age | Years | Contributions | End-of-Year Value |
| 25 | 1 | $2,000 | $2,145 | 25 | 1 | $0 | $0 |
| 26 | 2 | $2,000 | $4,444 | 26 | 2 | $0 | $0 |
| 27 | 3 | $2,000 | $6,910 | 27 | 3 | $0 | $0 |
| 28 | 4 | $2,000 | $9,554 | 28 | 4 | $0 | $0 |
| 29 | 5 | $2,000 | $12,389 | 29 | 5 | $0 | $0 |
| 30 | 6 | $2,000 | $15,430 | 30 | 6 | $0 | $0 |
| 31 | 7 | $2,000 | $18,680 | 31 | 7 | $0 | $0 |
| 32 | 8 | $2,000 | $22,185 | 32 | 8 | $0 | $0 |
| 33 | 9 | $2,000 | $25,934 | 33 | 9 | $0 | $0 |
| 34 | 10 | $2,000 | $29,953 | 34 | 10 | $0 | $0 |
| 35 | 11 | $0 | $32,118 | 35 | 11 | $2,000 | $2,145 |
| 36 | 12 | $0 | $34,440 | 36 | 12 | $2,000 | $4,445 |
| 37 | 13 | $0 | $36,930 | 37 | 13 | $2,000 | $6,910 |

Continued

**Table 7-1:** **The Timing of Your Investment Influences Your Return** *(continued)*

| Mary Anne | | | | Karl | | | |
|---|---|---|---|---|---|---|---|
| Age | Years | Contributions | End-of-Year Value | Age | Years | Contributions | End-of-Year Value |
| 38 | 14 | $0 | $39,598 | 38 | 14 | $2,000 | $9,554 |
| 39 | 15 | $0 | $42,462 | 39 | 15 | $2,000 | $12,390 |
| 40 | 16 | $0 | $45,532 | 40 | 16 | $2,000 | $15,430 |
| 41 | 17 | $0 | $48,823 | 41 | 17 | $2,000 | $18,690 |
| 42 | 18 | $0 | $52,353 | 42 | 18 | $2,000 | $22,185 |
| 43 | 19 | $0 | $56,137 | 43 | 19 | $2,000 | $25,934 |
| 44 | 20 | $0 | $60,195 | 44 | 20 | $2,000 | $29,953 |
| 45 | 21 | $0 | $64,547 | 45 | 21 | $2,000 | $34,263 |
| 46 | 22 | $0 | $69,213 | 46 | 22 | $2,000 | $38,884 |
| 47 | 23 | $0 | $74,216 | 47 | 23 | $2,000 | $43,840 |
| 48 | 24 | $0 | $79,582 | 48 | 24 | $2,000 | $49,154 |
| 49 | 25 | $0 | $85,334 | 49 | 25 | $2,000 | $54,851 |
| 50 | 26 | $0 | $91,503 | 50 | 26 | $2,000 | $60,961 |
| 51 | 27 | $0 | $98,118 | 51 | 27 | $2,000 | $67,513 |
| 52 | 28 | $0 | $105,221 | 52 | 28 | $2,000 | $74,538 |

| ***Mary Anne*** | | | | ***Karl*** | | | |
|---|---|---|---|---|---|---|---|
| ***Age*** | ***Years*** | ***Contributions*** | ***End-of-Year Value*** | ***Age*** | ***Years*** | ***Contributions*** | ***End-of-Year Value*** |
| 53 | 29 | $0 | $112,817 | 53 | 29 | $2,000 | $82,070 |
| 54 | 30 | $0 | $120,972 | 54 | 30 | $2,000 | $90,148 |
| 55 | 31 | $0 | $129,717 | 55 | 31 | $2,000 | $98,810 |
| 56 | 32 | $0 | $139,094 | 56 | 32 | $2,000 | $108,097 |
| 57 | 33 | $0 | $149,150 | 57 | 33 | $2,000 | $118,056 |
| 58 | 34 | $0 | $159,932 | 58 | 34 | $2,000 | $128,735 |
| 59 | 35 | $0 | $171,493 | 59 | 35 | $2,000 | $140,187 |
| 60 | 36 | $0 | $183,890 | 60 | 36 | $2,000 | $152,464 |
| 61 | 37 | $0 | $197,184 | 61 | 37 | $2,000 | $165,631 |
| 62 | 38 | $0 | $211,438 | 62 | 38 | $2,000 | $179,749 |
| 63 | 39 | $0 | $226,723 | 63 | 39 | $2,000 | $194,887 |
| 64 | 40 | $0 | $243,113 | 64 | 40 | $2,000 | $211,121 |
| 65 | 41 | $0 | $260,690 | 65 | 41 | $2,000 | $228,530 |
| Value at retirement: $260,690 | | | | Value at retirement: $228,530 | | | |
| Minus total contributions: $20,000 | | | | Minus total contributions: $62,000 | | | |
| Net earnings: $240,690 | | | | Net earnings: $166,530 | | | |

By waiting ten years, Karl had to put in more than three times as much money as Mary Anne, and he still held an investment worth almost 12 percent less than hers. When they turned 65, Mary Anne's investment had increased by $17,577 over the preceding year, even though she added nothing to her fund. Karl's fund had increased by $17,409, but he added $2,000 to his fund during that year.

Even if you're not as young as Karl and Mary Anne when you start investing, the younger you are, the more money you'll have when you retire, and the less money will have to come out of your paycheck.

If you don't want to spend your life researching and making decisions about your investments, a fund that reinvests dividends may be the best choice for you. Because you'll never see a check for what your investment earns, you won't be tempted to divert it away from your retirement funding.

## Tracking Your Investments

*Tracking* is keeping records of how each of your investments is performing. Tracking may take a variety of forms, from simple lists to charts and graphs. People learn in different ways, so choose the form that makes it easiest for you to get quick and clear answers to your questions.

You can use a simple form like the following worksheet to track the performance of your mutual fund investments. You can use this information elsewhere to figure your gains (or losses) as adjusted for inflation, taxes, and so on (although this example makes no such adjustments).

**My Mutual Fund Record**

Date: _____

Fund name: _____

Fund type: _____

Date purchased: _____

Number of shares purchased: _____

Purchase price per share: _____

Total cost: _____

Date shares reinvested: _____

Current number of shares: _____

Current price per share: _____

Current value: _____

Dividend paid: _____

Date sold: _____

Number of shares sold: _____

Money received: _____

Profit (Loss): _____

Total annual management fees: _____

Keep the same kind of record for your stock investments. The following worksheet shows you how to record information that's appropriate to stock purchases and sales.

**My Stock Record**

Date: _____

Stock name: _____

Date purchased: _____

Number of shares purchased: _____

Price per share: _____

Total cost: _____

Stock split date: _____

Current number of shares: _____

Current price per share: _____

Current value: _____

Date sold: _____

Number of shares sold: _____

Money received: _____

Profit (Loss): _____

Perhaps you decided to invest in bonds. The information you need to record is slightly different, as shown in the following worksheet.

**My Bond Record**

Date: _____

Name of bond: _____

Bond number or book entry number: _____

Bond type: _____

Bond price: _____

Date of purchase: _____

Sale/Maturity date: _____

Current interest yield: _____

Tax status: _____

Conversion callable features: _____

Net sales price: _____

Net gain/loss: _____

If a bond is called, it stops earning interest on the call date. Make sure to redeem a called bond by the call date.

If you use a personal accounting software package such as Quicken, Budget, or Microsoft Money, keeping track of your investments is even easier. Some of the available features are

- The ability to track individual investments

- The ability to keep track of entire portfolios

- Graphs showing the history of each of your investments

- Registers showing every transaction for a portfolio

You can create any of these categories on paper, but the software makes record-keeping much easier. For example, you can update your Share Balance or Cash Balance records. Instead of having to create a transaction to reflect the new number of shares held, you can make these adjustments directly on the balance sheet.

Quicken offers its own Mutual Fund Finder. You can choose criteria based on the investment questions that you answered earlier in this chapter. After you decide what you want from your investment instrument, the Mutual Fund Finder lists those funds that meet your needs. You can even rank funds so that the information is in an even more useful form.

The Internet is a great source of data on which to make your decisions. You can download financial news, price updates for instruments in your portfolio, and historical data about your stocks (or ones that you're interested in buying).

## Why you do it

Tracking the performance of your investments keeps you current on trends involving your own investments and in the market as a whole. Efficient investing, like budgeting, relies on good information.

In every other part of your financial planning, you consider how your decisions will impact your income tax bill. That consideration is at least as important in investing. Unlike wages, you control when you pay taxes on your investments by the types of investments you choose. Using software to insert new data and see the overall impact makes it easier to track — and makes ignoring it less acceptable.

## How you do it

Probably the number one rule is to read all the information that the companies with which you hold mutual funds, stocks, and bonds send to you. Online information is fine, but the literature that you get directly from the companies contains information that, apart from finances, defines how you want to make decisions.

In addition to what comes in the mail, you can check your newspaper to compare your fund with others. This information, in the words of musician Kenny Rogers, helps you "know when to hold 'em and know when to fold 'em."

# ONCE YOU'VE REACHED YOUR FIRST GOAL

## IN THIS CHAPTER

- Enjoying the fruits of your victory over financial indecision

- Accounting for changes in your lifestyle and your income

- Using the reinforcement from your past fiscal victories to stay on course

Doesn't it feel good to know where your money is going? Aren't you enjoying all the energy that you're *not* spending on worrying about money? Isn't it nice to have a picture of your financial future?

When you started on this journey, you spent a lot of time gathering information. Then you had to make decisions — a *lot* of decisions — about the information you gathered. The fact that you're in Chapter 8 means that you saw the value of those exercises, you did them, and you have your budget firmly in control.

But a budget isn't a static thing. As you change, your needs will change, and so must your budget. This chapter talks about how to maintain and make adjustments to your budget so that you can deal with those changes.

## Enjoying the Fruits of Your Frugality

If you've planned well, whatever you want is now in your budget. If you don't believe that, walk through the following process:

1. You want to take a three-week trip to Paris. You look at your budget. You have plenty of money in your savings account. Unfortunately, that's not your vacation savings account, and you don't have enough in your vacation account. You can pay for your flight to and from the City of Light, and even for a hotel. But you don't have enough left to eat, pay admission to the museums, or even ride the Metro. Realizing that you need to regroup, you go on to Step 2.

2. If you take the same amount and stay in Paris for only two weeks, you can eat and see the sights, too. You won't be able to eat well (in Paris!), and you won't be able to see all the sights, but you'll still have a nice vacation. But you wonder whether a skimpy trip without much in the way of luxuries is what you want. So you survey other choices. Go on to Step 3.

3. You could go to Paris for one week. Doing so would move enough money from your hotel fund to your food and entertainment fund to give you a first-class vacation. One drawback is that the transportation time and cost are the same whether you stay for one week or three. Keep a one-week trip as an option and go on to Step 4.

4. Looking closer to home, you find Montreal, Canada. They speak French there. They have museums. They have great restaurants. Your cousin Fred will put you up for your stay.

You now have two alternatives that can meet at least part of your goal. No robbing Peter to pay Paul. No borrowing from your long-term savings for a short-term treat. No stress. And you still get to choose between one week in Paris and three weeks in Montreal.

This is just one simple example of how you should be making financial decisions now. Every choice has a benefit, and you know what that benefit is. Every choice has a negative side, too, and you are aware of that side as well. After finishing all those surveys about your financial picture and making all those choices based on your personal alternatives, good financial decisions are now at your fingertips.

# Rebudgeting for Change

Where does rebudgeting come in? You choose to change your budget either when you're financially uncomfortable or when a major change in your life impacts your financial situation. (The vacation example is not a case of rebudgeting; it's a reallocation of funds that you've already budgeted.)

### What should I do with that raise?

You got a raise, and you're going to spend it. Isn't that what a raise is for? The question is, how are you going to spend it? Review your budget to identify likely items to which you may want to apply that new money:

- Buy new furniture

- Go on vacation or upgrade your vacation

- Invest

- Pay down your mortgage early

- Pay off old debts

- Make a gift to your church or alma mater

- Start a college fund for your children

- Go back to school yourself

- Contract for maid service

The last choice may have surprised you, but remember that you're not supposed to deny yourself *everything*. You're just supposed to make a decision about every financial move you make and be aware of the pluses and minuses of each decision.

Explore the maid idea, for example. Do you have a hobby that you'd like to turn into a business, but you're already working full-time? Hiring a maid could free enough time for you to follow your dream. Over the long term, will having a maid allow you to make more money than you pay for her services?

Or maybe you just hate cleaning. You earned the money, so you can make the decision to have the cleaning done for you if you want to. It's okay to make a decision just because it's something you want, as long as you know what alternatives you're choosing to do without.

If you use the extra money in your paycheck to pay for a short-term goal, such as buying new furniture or going on vacation, either you can decide now what you want to do with the extra money after you meet the short-term goal, or you can wait until you meet that goal and then go through the decision-making process again.

If you decide on a long-term goal, you still have decisions to make. For example, if the money is going into investments, will you choose risky or safe investments? Your previous work should have put you in good stead to make wise decisions that will lead to a stronger financial future.

What you can't do is not make a decision. Your money will be gone, and you either won't know where it went or you'll have buyer's remorse because you'll wish that you'd spent it on something else.

## We're having a baby!

As happy as the news of a baby on the way is for couples, it's also a cause for panic among the ill-prepared. One of the first questions they may ask is, "How are we going to pay for this?"

Even if the baby is a surprise, you're prepared to reorganize your funds and reprioritize your goals quickly because you have a budget and a savings plan. You know where all your money is going, and you've identified opportunities for cutting more spending or earning extra income. Therefore, you have everything you need to make a good decision about reallocating your funds to meet your new obligations.

Having a baby is more than just hugs and diapers. Using the evaluation skills that you've developed by reading this book, you need to make decisions about other changes, such as

- How are you going to pay the hospital bills? (Or are you going to use a midwife?)

- Do you need more insurance?

- Do you need larger housing? If not now, when in the future?

- How are you going to pay for the ongoing costs of diapers, clothing, food, healthcare, child care, schooling, summer camps, sports, proms, weddings, and all the rest?

And what a lucky baby! From her first allowance, you'll be teaching her the same good budgeting skills that you've learned.

## Let's buy a house!

The time has come. You set up a fund to save for a down payment on a home. You decided how much you can afford to pay for your new home, so you've already saved a 20 percent down payment so that you can get the lowest mortgage interest rates. Now you get to make specific decisions about where you'll live.

Any real estate office will have forms to help you decide what you want in a house. Your local library also should have plenty of information about home buying.

The best-laid plans will go awry. As a good/bad example: Marie got the house she wanted when the previous buyers backed out. Those buyers wanted to use the finished basement as a den. The problem was that their furniture was too tall to go down the basement stairs. Investigate *everything* about your purchase. Be flexible. Be prepared.

The down payment is only the first piece of the buying puzzle. To avoid unpleasant financial surprises, you also need to make sure that you have enough money to cover

■ Moving expenses

■ Utility deposits

■ Points and other closing cost paid to the lender and due at closing

■ Monthly mortgage payments

■ Property taxes

■ Homeowner's insurance

■ Redecorating and/or repair expenses

Saving money is a foundation of budgeting and having a savings/financial plan. If you concentrate too much on the dollar sign and not enough on quality, however, you could be in for some nasty financial surprises. This doesn't mean that you need to pay top dollar, but asking others for recommendations can help you stay out of the quicksand.

Areas in which you should shop for bargains but be very careful in your choices include the following:

■ Movers (Get recommendations from people who have been happy with their movers.)

■ Painting and decorating supplies (Applying bad paint takes the same amount of time and energy as applying good paint.)

- Cleaning supplies (Paying more doesn't mean that the product cleans better.)

- Packing materials (Skimping here will lead to breakage.)

- Appliances (If you don't have all the appliances you need, figure out what you can do without for the time being so that you can buy the best quality for your current needs.)

## Retaining Your Good Habits

The Introduction to this book promised you that if you gathered the information requested and made step-by-step decisions, the end result would be a financial plan that enables you to reach your short-term, mid-term, and long-term goals.

Because you're reading this section, I know that you followed the plan. You recognize that the steps you took have constructed a sound, firm financial plan. This is a good time to review all your "homework." To keep up your good habits, review your budget, your investment records, your net worth statement, and your personal property inventory.

Did you find that this review offered any real surprises? Probably not. You've been using these records all along. What you should do is appreciate how much in-depth knowledge you have about your financial affairs. That hard data, along with your knowledge of your saving and spending personalities, gives you the background to make future decisions without having to go through the entire process again. You get to enjoy the time you save and the stress you avoid.

Knowing the advantages that you've gained from your previous work ensures that you'll continue using the process outlined in this book to keep your financial records up-to-date.

What changes can you expect? As you move through life, you'll meet your short-term goals, and what were mid-term goals will become short-term goals. As you recognize your spending personality and make choices that make the most of your strengths and accommodate your weaknesses, your spending personality itself will evolve. Recognizing those changes, you'll want to reevaluate your spending personality periodically so that you can base future decisions on current information.

Likewise, your saving and investing personality will change. Part of the change will come because, as you age and either meet or fail to meet your goals, how you feel about saving and investing will change. Revisit the section in Chapter 7 on recognizing your saving personality and redefine your saving personality so that you can base future decisions on your updated profile.

You know how difficult breaking a bad habit can be. Every time you go back to the bad habit, that habit becomes even stronger. Luckily, the same is true of good habits. Take a minute to think of a good habit that you exercise without even thinking about it. For example, you may never litter because you were taught not to litter when you were very young. Do you say "Please" and "Thank you"? You probably don't even think of these things or give yourself credit for them.

The habit of making smart financial planning and spending decisions that you learned from this book will become stronger and stronger as you practice it. If you give yourself credit for all that you've accomplished, you'll want to continue those good habits.

# CLIFFSNOTES REVIEW

Use this CliffsNotes Review to practice what you've learned in this book and to build your confidence in doing the job right the first time. After you work through the review questions, the problem-solving exercises, and the fun and useful scenarios and practice project, you're well on your way to achieving your goal of creating and using a budget.

## Q&A

**1.** What is compounding?

   **a.** The accrual of interest on a debt

   **b.** Interest paid on interest

   **c.** The complicated nature of budgeting

**2.** True or False: You can do your banking online.

**3.** Fixed expenses include

   **a.** Healthcare, housing, and transportation

   **b.** Housing, food, and entertainment

   **c.** Clothing, movies, and CDs

**4.** List three good financial habits that you have already established.

   1) _____

   2) _____

   3) _____

**5.** Name your most common spending trigger.

   _____

**6.** True or False: You should buy an item if you have a coupon for it, whether or not you really need it.

**7.** The following is a good way to live on less:

   **a.** Stop eating breakfast every day

   **b.** Buy a bagel and a cup of gourmet coffee on your way to work

   **c.** Take your lunch to work rather than go out to eat

**8.** Financial advisers recommend that no more than _____ percent of your net income be dedicated to paying your consumer debt.

    **a.** 10

    **b.** 20

    **c.** 30

**9.** When you're in debt, your best strategy for spending is to

    **a.** Continue using your credit cards, even if you're already carrying a balance

    **b.** Borrow money from your friends

    **c.** Pay off your highest-interest debts first

**10.** Name three future goals that you may need to rebudget for.

    1) _____

    2) _____

    3) _____

**Answers:** (1) b. (2) True. (3) a. (4) Answers will vary. (5) Answers will vary. (6) False. (7) c. (8) b. (9) c. (10) Answers will vary.

## Scenario

You decide that you want to purchase a new car in one year. To ensure that you have enough money for a down payment, you should change your budget by_____

_____

**Answer:** Figure out how much you need to save per month for the down payment, and then add that amount as a fixed expense in your budget.

## Consider This

■ Did you know that the little purchases that you don't even think about can do the worst damage to your budget? See Chapter 2 for more information.

■   Did you know that you can rack up a lot of debt quickly by using credit cards and not paying off the balances each month? See Chapter 6 to find out how to tackle your debt.

■   Did you know that you can buy anything you want if you just put it into your budget and have the patience to save up the money you need? See Chapter 3 for instructions for creating a budget and Chapter 4 for tips on how to stick to it.

■   Did you know that you can cut your expenses and not "do without"? See Chapter 5 for expense-reducing ideas.

## Practice Project

1. Track your spending on food, including snacks and soft drinks from vending machines, for one week. For tips on keeping a spending diary, see Chapter 2.

2. At the end of each week, identify which expenditures you could have done without, and tally how much those expenditures cost.

3. Make a list of the goals you could have come closer to achieving by putting the money you identified in Step 2 toward them rather than spending it on junk food, trinkets, and the like.

4. Remember this exercise the next time you're about to make a purchase without thinking about the financial consequences of it!

# CLIFFSNOTES RESOURCE CENTER

Now that you have the basics well in hand, you'll want to fine-tune your budgeting and savings skills. CliffsNotes Resource Center guides you to the best of the best — links to the best information in print and online about budgeting and saving. These terrific resources are available at your favorite bookstore and on the Internet. When you go online, make your first stop at www.cliffsnotes.com, where you'll find an even bigger CliffsNotes Resource Center.

## Books

This CliffsNotes book is one of many great books that can help you master budgeting, saving, and investing. For some great next-step books, start with these other publications:

- **Banking Online For Dummies**, by Paul A. Murphy. This book helps you explore your options, including viewing which checks have cleared, finding your current balance, and paying bills online. You can also discover the differences among the popular software programs Microsoft Money, Managing Your Money, and Quicken, and explore online security issues. IDG Books Worldwide, Inc., $24.99.

- **CliffsNotes Investing for the First Time**, by Tracey Longo. This book shows you how to start investing your hard-earned and hard-saved dollars, whether you want to play it safe or you're willing to take risks in hopes of big returns. IDG Books Worldwide, Inc., $8.99.

- **Mortgages For Dummies**, by Eric Tyson and Ray Brown. If a new house is in your budget, this book can tell you everything you need to know, from finding your dream house to getting a mortgage. IDG Books Worldwide, Inc., $16.99.

- **Mutual Funds For Dummies**, by Eric Tyson. This book tells you about the world of investing in mutual funds, from researching funds to using funds in retirement planning. IDG Books Worldwide, Inc., $16.99.

It's easy to find books published by IDG Books Worldwide, Inc. You can find them in your favorite bookstores near you and on the Internet. We also have three Web sites that you can use to read about our entire line of all the books we publish:

- www.cliffsnotes.com
- www.dummies.com
- www.idgbooks.com

# Internet

The Internet contains many sites that will help you make the most of your budgeting and financial decisions. Check out these Web sites for more information:

- **Manage Your Money, www.aarp.org/money/home.html** — Manage Your Money is one of the most popular personal finance software packages. Check out the latest offerings here.

- **BestRate, www.bestrate.com** — This site enables you to compare lender rates and fees, use a mortgage calculator, get a credit report, explore insurance costs, and find a contractor. It also has information about the stock market and credit cards.

- **The Motley Fool, www.fool.com** — The Motley Fool offers easily understandable information about investing and investment clubs, tracking your stock portfolio (real or mock), using credit cards responsibly, budgeting, and other aspects of personal finance. Grow wise along with your fellow befuddled would-be financial planners.

- **Intuit, www.intuit.com** — Learn all that Quicken personal finance and investing software has to offer you at this site.

- **Microsoft, www.microsoft.com** — If you're thinking of buying Microsoft Money to track your budgeting, checkbook, and investments — and to be able to do it online — get your information here.

- **Moneyminded, www.moneyminded.com** — Primarily women-centered, this site has advice that is on target for anyone. It offers information about everything from budgets to money personality to spending habits to investing — with some money-makeover tips thrown in for good measure.

- **Registered Financial Planners Institute, www.rfpi.com** — Visit the site of the Registered Financial Planners Institute to get information about insurance agents, attorneys, loan officers, real estate agents, certified public accountants, bankers, stock brokers, and other similar professionals. Registered members have met stringent educational requirements.

- **washingtonpost.com Personal Finance, www.washingtonpost.com/wp-srv/business/yrmoney.htm** — Research mutual funds with Morningstar, track your stocks, find tax tips, get advice from the experts, and more from this area of *The Washington Post*'s site.

Next time you're on the Internet, don't forget to drop by www.cliffsnotes.com. We created an online Resource Center that you can use today, tomorrow, and beyond.

## Magazines & Other Media

Try the following publications for additional, current information about the world of personal finance:

- **Kiplinger's Personal Finance Magazine (www.kiplinger.com/magazine)** can help you understand spending and saving, working and retiring, and the other parts of your financial life and planning.

- **Money Magazine (www.pathfinder.com/money)** covers everything from evaluating brokers to moving your money from pricey stocks to less expensive ones so that you have continuous growth in your portfolio. Not for novices, but you don't have to be a pro, either.

- **Smart Money Magazine (www.smartmoney.com)** is comprehensive, covering everything from stock watches to stock recommendations. Like anything else, you get out what you put in. There's a lot of information here, but this site can serve as your online personal financial instructor.

## Send Us Your Favorite Tips

In your quest for learning, have you ever experienced that sublime moment when you figure out a trick that saves time or trouble? Perhaps you realized you were taking ten steps to accomplish something that could have taken two. Or you found a little-known workaround that gets great results. If you've discovered a useful tip that helped you budget more effectively and you'd like to share it, the CliffsNotes staff would love to hear from you. Go to our Web site at www.cliffsnotes.com and click the Talk to Us button.

If we select your tip, we may publish it as part of CliffsNotes Daily, our exciting, free e-mail newsletter. To find out more or to subscribe to a newsletter, go to **www.cliffsnotes .com** on the Web.

# INDEX

## NUMBERS AND SYMBOLS

401(k) plans, 88

## A

accountants, 54
additional income, 67
alternatives to spending, 59
annual fees, 30
antiques, as assets, 7
appliances wearing out, 55
asking for a raise, 68
assets, accumulating, 9
assets, tracking, 6
ATM fees, 30
automatic payments, 18
Automobiles
    loans, 79
    maintenance, 32

## B

babies, impact on budget, 104
balanced portfolios, 86
bank accounts
    consolidating, 6
    fees, 6, 30
    high interest, 6
    records, 18
*Banking Online For Dummies*, 112
bankruptcies, 81
banks, 6
bartering, 61
bartering clubs, 62
being realistic, 44
below-minimum balance fees, 30
below-minimum use fees, 30
boats, down payments, 11
bonds, 7, 98
bonds, called, 99
borrowing, 60
budget, creating, 27
budget software, 19, 99
budget worksheets, 20, 39
budgeting software, 19, 38
budgeting, benefits of, 10
budgets, benefits of, 15
budgets, failing to use and revise, 46
budgets, realistic, 44
budgets, setting up basic, 38
budgets, sticking to, 45
buying decisions, 26

## C

capital value accounts, 90
career changes, impact on goals, 12
catalog shopping, 31
cautious buyers, 25
CDs. *See* certificates of deposit, 88
celebration, as spending trigger, 48
certificates of deposit, 6, 87
change of terms inserts from banks, credit
    card companies, etc., 30
charitable contributions, 27
checking accounts, 5
children, 52
Christmas Club accounts, 6
CliffsNotes Daily, 3, 116
CliffsNotes Investing for the First Time, 112
CliffsNotes Resource Center, 112
CliffsNotes Review, 109
CliffsNotes Web site, 3
co-owning, 60
collectibles, as assets, 7
college fund, child's, 10
company gyms, 66
competition, as spending trigger, 48
compounding, 6, 11, 14
consolidation loans, 81
consumer debt, 72
coupons, 63
credit and loan payments, 23
credit cards
    fees, 30
    skipping a payment, 56
    statements, 19
credit counseling services, 75
credit ratings, 78
credit unions, 6
current financial situation, determining, 5

## D

debt, avoiding new, 76
debt-repayment plan, 70
debts, paying off, 67
defaults, 81
deferring payments, 77
delivery charges, 31
department store credit cards, 75
depression, as spending trigger, 47
desire to impress someone, as spending
    trigger, 48
determining current financial status, 5
determining nonessential expenses, 28
discipline, importance of, 45
discount stores, 66
discretionary income, 28
diversification, 89
dividends accounts, 90
dividends, reinvesting, 96
down payments, accumulating, 10

# COMING SOON FROM CLIFFSNOTES

Online Shopping

HTML

Choosing a PC

Beginning Programming

Careers

Windows 98 Home Networking

eBay Online Auctions

PC Upgrade and Repair

Business

Microsoft Word 2000

Microsoft PowerPoint 2000

Finance

Microsoft Outlook 2000

Digital Photography

Palm Computing

Investing

Windows 2000

Online Research

IDG BOOKS WORLDWIDE

# COMING SOON FROM CLIFFSNOTES
## *Buying and Selling on eBay*

Have you ever experienced the thrill of finding an incredible bargain at a specialty store or been amazed at what people are willing to pay for things that you might toss in the garbage? If so, then you'll want to learn about eBay — the hottest auction site on the Internet. And CliffsNotes *Buying and Selling on eBay* is the shortest distance to eBay proficiency. You'll learn how to:

- Find what you're looking for, from antique toys to classic cars

- Watch the auctions strategically and place bids at the right time

- Sell items online at the eBay site

- Make the items you sell attractive to prospective bidders

- Protect yourself from fraud

Here's an example of how the step-by-step CliffsNotes learning process simplifies placing a bid at eBay:

**1.** Scroll to the Web page form that is located at the bottom of the page on which the auction item itself is presented.

**2.** Enter your registered eBay username and password and enter the amount you want to bid. A Web page appears that lets you review your bid before you actually submit it to eBay. After you're satisfied with your bid, click the Place Bid button.

**3.** Click the Back button on your browser until you return to the auction listing page. Then choose⇨Reload (Netscape Navigator) or View⇨Refresh (Microsoft Internet Explorer) to reload the Web page information. Your new high bid appears on the Web page, and your name appears as the high bidder.